"Often hiding behind the platitudes of 'doing good' at meetings like the World Economic Forum, private capital investors are laying waste to the environment and facilitating the growing inequality that leaves ever greater numbers of people living in poverty. When we focus on these 'Titans of Capital' and understand how they use financial power to mold our lives, we may be able to find sustainable alternatives for the long-term economic and environmental health and human well-being most of us crave. *Titans* is an essential book for addressing humanity's current crisis and for re-evaluating our acquiescence to the financiers who currently run the world."
—ROBIN ANDERSEN, Professor Emerita of Communication and Media Studies, Fordham University

"With *Titans of Capital*, Professor Peter Phillips has produced a masterful follow-up to *Giants: The Global Power Elite*. This is a very necessary sequel because all of the alarming trends that Phillips identified in 2018 have only accelerated. As *Titans* points out, there were nearly twice as many trillion-dollar capital management firms in 2022 compared to 2017. At the same time, *Titans* has a narrower focus. . . . Phillips focuses on an even tighter core of 117 persons who sit on the executive boards of the top ten capital management firms. If you want to know about who is running the world on behalf of the global oligarchy of wealth, read *Titans of Capital*!"
—AARON GOOD, author of *American Exception: Empire and the Deep State*

"Some years ago, I wrote a short endorsement of Peter Phillips's excellent book *Giants: The Global Power Elite*. His new book, *Titans of Capital*, is even better, making connections between corporate capital and almost all the institutions of social life globally—a textbook of capitalism's deficiencies."
—LESLIE SKLAIR, Professor Emeritus of Sociology, London School of Economics

TITANS
OF CAPITAL

HOW CONCENTRATED WEALTH
THREATENS HUMANITY

PETER PHILLIPS

FOREWORD BY
DAN KOVALIK

THE CENSORED
— PRESS —

SEVEN STORIES

FAIR OAKS, CA • NEW YORK

The Censored Press　　　　Seven Stories Press
PO Box 1177　　　　　　　140 Watts Street
Fair Oaks, CA 95628　　　　New York, NY 10013
censoredpress.org　　　　　sevenstories.com

Library of Congress Cataloging-in-Publication Data is on file.

ISBN 978-1-64421-433-6 (paperback)
ISBN 978-1-64421-434-3 (ebook)

College professors and high school and middle school teachers may order free examination copies of Seven Stories Press titles. Visit https://www.sevenstories.com/pg/resources-academics or email academic@sevenstories.com.

Printed in the United States of America

9 8 7 6 5 4 3 2 1

DEDICATION

TO VETERANS FOR PEACE, an organization of military veterans and allies whose collective efforts build a culture of peace worldwide. VFP has 140 chapters in the US and six other countries.

Veterans For Peace Chapter 63 in Albuquerque, New Mexico has been dedicated to opposing the construction of nuclear weapons in our state and ending all wars.

Chapter 63's members include: Bill Tiwald, Barbara Tiwald, Robert Anderson, Charles Powell, Sally-Alice Thompson, Mandy Pino, Willard Hunter, John E. Wilks III, Bear Albrecht, Kathy Albrecht, Art Ratcliffe, Tom Delehanty, Arla Ertz, Don Kimball, Jack Turner, Ravi Wadhwani, Mike Gallagher, Penelope Mainz, Laura Martin, Paul Pino, Dan Shelton, and Peter Phillips.

CONTENTS

FOREWORD
by Dan Kovalik

In *Titans of Capital*, Peter Phillips names the world's top ten investment management firms controlling a huge portion of humanity's wealth—close to $50 trillion—and the 117 individuals who serve on these firms' executive boards. These businesses and individuals constitute the international ruling class, to use Marxist terms, whose decisions impact nearly every facet of our lives. And they make these judgments in their own interest while claiming that they operate in the interest of all humanity.

Although seven of the top ten investment firms are based in the United States—and the other three in Europe—these entities owe no allegiance to any nation, only to themselves and their shareholders.

Political thinker and writer Michael Parenti once asked rhetorically, "What do the capitalists want?" His answer, quite simply: "Everything!" They want all the world's wealth and riches for themselves, and every choice they make comes back to that. And while the capitalist ruling class at least used to create something of value in the process of making their wealth—for example, by managing the workers who made steel, cars, appliances, railroads, and so forth—now the primary means of making profit is through finance. That is, through the process of making money from money rather than through industry, which requires investing profits back into productive pursuits. This financialization of the economy focuses on short-term gain while sacrificing long-term stability and growth. Indeed, the new economic system controlled by these superrich companies and their managers thrives on chaos and instability.

The ruling class will never let a good crisis go to waste, seizing upon every disaster to make profit. A good example of this is the recent COVID-19 pandemic. In the midst of it, the superrich got even richer, and the poor got proportionally poorer. As US senator Elizabeth Warren explained:

> Pre-pandemic, the wealth gap between the wealthiest and the poorest Americans was already wider than ever. But the coronavirus and the economic crisis that followed have made that gap even worse. While millions of Americans remain unemployed and families are struggling to keep a roof over their heads and food on the table, billionaire wealth has grown to $4.2 trillion, 40% higher than before the COVID crisis began.[1]

Here, Peter Phillips explains that the "Titans of Capital," the leaders of the world's largest investment firms, were among those that made a killing during the pandemic, while the poor were simply killed. As he relates:

> [Extreme poverty] was slowly declining during the three decades preceding the pandemic, but this trend

---

1. "It's Time for a Wealth Tax," Warren for Senate, accessed September 6, 2023.

was reversed in 2020, after COVID-19 spread. At that point, inequality was amplified as wealth concentration accelerated for the 1 percent and declined for the 99 percent, forcing 180 million more people into extreme poverty. Developing countries, women, and ethnic minorities were hardest hit by the pandemic. The number of people in extreme poverty rose to more than 700 million. According to the World Bank, the rate of global extreme poverty reached 9.3 percent in 2020, up from 8.4 percent in 2019.

This is an extraordinary reallocation of wealth upward—quite possibly the greatest in all human history. And, of course, this was not by accident. Instead, the policies that were implemented, without any public debate, allegedly to deal with the pandemic, guaranteed that this would be the result. Those policies included, for example, lockdowns that shuttered mom-and-pop and other "informal" small businesses, while keeping Walmarts, Targets, and Amazon going as "essential businesses."

To celebrate their newfound wealth, and to parade it in front of the people they stole it from, billionaires including Elon Musk, Jeff Bezos, and Richard Branson took much-publicized victory laps in space while the proles were confined to quarters and barred from even going out to dinner. And we were told by the media that the superrich are in control and that we must simply grin and bear this for our own good and shun anyone who dares complain about the obvious injustice. The worst of the pharaohs would blush at such brazenness, but alas, this is the brave new world that the international capitalists have created for us.

Another example is the August 2023 destruction by fire of

the town of Lahaina, in Maui, Hawaii, which claimed the lives of at least ninety-seven people. Within days, outside real estate investors were swooping in to make cash offers to desperate Lahaina homeowners. Even the establishment press and government authorities characterized these maneuvers as "predatory."[1] Reuters highlighted one typical homeowner who was inundated with purchase offers after the horrible tragedy:

> Deborah Loeffler felt she could not lose much more after a wildfire destroyed the home in Maui where five generations of her family have lived, and a son died the same day on the U.S. mainland. Grieving and overwhelmed, Loeffler was soon beset by emails with unsolicited proposals to sell the Lahaina beachfront plot in Maui where her grandfather built their teal-green wooden home in the 1940s.
>
>   "It felt like we had vultures preying on us," said Loeffler, 69, a retired flight attendant.[2]

The land-grabbing attempts were so fast and furious that many began to suspect investors might have set the fire purposefully to create the very opportunity they were seizing upon.[3] These suspicions were fueled by the fact that the homeowners on the island had for years resisted attempts by speculators to buy their properties.

While there appears to be no good evidence as yet of such a conspiracy in the case of the Maui fire, there is no doubt

---

1. Megan Cerullo, "Maui Residents 'Disturbed' by Outside Realtors Offering Quick Cash for Land," CBS News, August 28, 2023.
2. Andrew Hay and Liliana Salgado, "Maui Wildfire Victims Fear Land Grab May Threaten Hawaiian Culture," Reuters, August 22, 2023.
3. Alex Oliveira, "Maui Wildfires Spark Conspiracy Theories about Space Lasers, Oprah Land Grabs and Suspicious Trees," *New York Post*, August 15, 2023, updated August 16, 2023.

that the finance capitalists who dominate our world are quite willing to create crises to achieve their wealth-grabbing goals. The best example of this is war—a quite lucrative type of crisis for the Titans of Capital. As George Orwell wrote in *1984*, "The war is not meant to be won; it is meant to be continuous." In the modern age, arms dealers and the firms that invest in them turn profits on sales of guns and ammunition in perpetuity.

Probably the best example of war profiteering was the US war in Afghanistan, which lasted twenty years, from September 2001 to August 30, 2021. After trillions of dollars spent and tens of thousands of lives lost, the US military mission accomplished the impressive feat of ousting the Taliban and replacing it with the Taliban. However, this Rube Goldberg machine of a conflict was great for the industry, which worked tirelessly to the bitter end to wring every ounce of profit from the war.

Beginning in February 2020, as the US military started to wind down its Afghanistan operations, defense contractors lobbied even more in efforts to extend the war's duration and assure one more round of huge contracts before the bonanza finally ended. The top five defense companies—Lockheed Martin, Boeing, Raytheon, General Dynamics, and Northrop Grumman—spent a combined $34.2 million in lobbying in the first half of 2021, added to about $33 million in the same period of 2020.[1] Raytheon spent more than $15.3 million on lobbying in 2021, the most of any defense contractor; Lockheed Martin was second, shelling out more than $14.4 million that year.[2] As Phillips notes, all of these defense contractors receive signifi-

---

1. Anna Massoglia and Julia Forrest, "Defense Contractors Spent Big in Afghanistan before the U.S. Left and the Taliban Took Control," OpenSecrets, August 20, 2021.
2. "Client Profile: Raytheon Technologies," OpenSecrets, accessed September 6, 2023; "Client Profile: Lockheed Martin," OpenSecrets, accessed September 6. 2023.

cant investments from the Titans of Capital. As OpenSecrets reported in August 2021:

> The Congressional Research Service found that the Defense Department also obligated more money on federal contracts during the 2020 fiscal year than all other government agencies combined with around 31% of its contracts going to the five companies.
>
> People with ties to the defense industry have also been in positions to influence decision-making about the withdrawal from Afghanistan—including Retired General Joseph F. Dunford and former Sen. Kelly Ayotte (R-N.H.), who are two of three co-chairs on the congressionally-chartered Afghanistan Study Group.
>
> The majority of plenary members on the Afghanistan Study Group, which advised President Joe Biden to extend the originally-negotiated May 1 deadline for withdrawing from Afghanistan, also have ties to the defense industry. A couple of those members include former President Donald Trump's principal deputy director of national intelligence, Susan M. Gordon, and Stephen J. Hadley, former President George W. Bush's deputy national security adviser.[1]

What we witness here is the power of the military-industrial complex, as President Dwight D. Eisenhower termed it, which dictates US foreign policy to its benefit without regard to the welfare of the Afghan people, the American taxpayer, or US military personnel.

This is the tail wagging the proverbial dog, which was also

---

1. Massoglia and Forrest, "Defense Contractors Spent Big in Afghanistan."

evident in conflicts such as the North Atlantic Treaty Organization's 2011 operation in Libya and in Ukraine today, where the US maneuvered the world into a conflict that has benefited the arms industry.[1] Defense manufacturers are making a killing on the war along with Titans of Capital, such as stakeholders of BlackRock—the biggest of the Titans—which has made deals with Ukraine's President Zelensky to oversee and benefit from the huge development opportunities that the war creates.[2] Zelensky's official statement quoted Charles Hatami, the head of BlackRock's Financial & Strategic Investors Group, who noted that the firm was "honored to be assisting the Ukrainian people by advising the government on the launch of the Ukraine Development Fund. The reconstruction of the country will create significant opportunity for investors to participate in rebuilding the economy."[3] And BlackRock made sure that it will benefit from this "opportunity." Again, the capitalists will never let a good crisis go to waste.

Titans of Capital points to the firms and individuals laying waste to the world in pursuit of unlimited profit. Knowing who these Titans are, we can then target them for protest and public outrage. And it is indeed these firms and individuals whose lives must be inconvenienced by protest. While this should be an obvious point, we often see quite the opposite. That is, we see activists who are concerned about the environment and global climate change attack great works of art and inconvenience fellow citizens—for example, by creating a ten-mile traffic jam when they set up a roadblock (on tribal land, by the way) leading to the 2023 Burning Man event in

---

1. Daniel Kovalik, "Libya & Creative Destruction," CounterPunch, November 21, 2012.
2. "President Holds Meeting with World's Largest Investment Company on Creation of Fund for Rebuilding Ukraine," President of Ukraine, May 5, 2023.
3. Ibid.

Nevada—instead of confronting the firms and individuals who constitute our class enemies as well as the enemies of humanity.[1] This kind of misdirected activism is not only ineffective but also counterproductive. It alienates people from struggles they might otherwise embrace. The change we seek will only come when politically concerned people, informed by the gross inequalities documented in *Titans of Capital*, undertake direct activism.

1. Doha Madani, "Climate Change Activists Who Blockaded Burning Man Accuse Police of Excessive Force," NBC News, August 29, 2023.

INTRODUCTION

Titans of Capital updates and expands my earlier book *Giants: The Global Power Elite* (2018). *Giants* identified the 199 directors of the world's seventeen top asset management companies, which between them managed more than $41.1 trillion in wealth. Now, five years later, in *Titans of Capital*, I examine the ongoing rapid concentration of global capital and how fewer and larger companies now manage the excess financial wealth for the .05 percent (forty million) richest people in the world. As a political sociologist, I pose three research questions: To what extent do the wealthy influence—or even dominate—decision-making that affects all of us in society? Who are the most powerful people? And how does the process of influence or domination work?

Capitalism protects private ownership of property, business, and personal wealth. Governments control the legal and policing mechanisms that ensure wealth remains privately owned and that, to varying degrees, allow concentrated wealth to be used to amass even greater wealth. I review the academic research that addresses these sociological questions and contribute new research that offers a more in-depth analysis of the socioeconomic structures that facilitate massive wealth concentration and its inevitable worldwide consequences, including growing inequality, grinding poverty, and environmental destruction. My work now covers changes over five years that demonstrate how individuals and networked groups have evolved over time, thereby allowing me the opportunity for a macroanalysis of how national and transnational elites—whom I call Titans—mold the world to their liking.

Yes, the upper elites, who are one-twentieth of 1 percent (0.05) of the world's population, get richer, and the rest of us struggle to get by. More than half of the world's population lives in semipoverty, tormented by combinations of poor nutrition, homelessness or the threat of it, and inadequate health care. Sociologically, current global trends mean an even greater concentration of wealth, resources, and power in the hands of .05 percent of the world's population—and increasingly scarce resources and influence for the rest of us. Decisions made by elites regarding investments and economic policies affect the entire world, but not always for the better. The global consequences of extreme wealth inequality include wars and threats of war, repressed human rights and due processes, and environmental devastation. We are in a crisis of humanity, which William I. Robinson, a sociologist at the University of California, Santa Barbara, describes as a threat to the survival of our species and all living things.[1] Were nuclear war to become a reality rather than just a threat, most life on earth would be destroyed; meanwhile, the somewhat slower destruction of the environment poses similar dangers—many of which could occur within the life expectancy range of most humans living on Earth today.

In *Giants: The Global Power Elite,* I examined the seventeen capital management firms that controlled more than $1 trillion in investment funds in 2017. These seventeen firms collectively

---

1. William I. Robinson, *Global Capitalism and the Crisis of Humanity* (Cambridge: Cambridge University Press, 2014).

managed $41.1 trillion in investment capital in 2017 (one tril-
lion is one thousand billion). To visualize how much money
this is, consider the following: If one were to spend $40 per
second, it would take 289 days to spend $1 billion. And that's
at a spending rate of almost $3.45 million per day. At the same
rate of $40 per second, it would take 792.5 years to go through
$1 trillion. That amount would be like giving more than $3,000
to every person living in the US, or about $4,800 to every indi-
vidual in the US over the age of eighteen.[1]

GIANTS: TOP ASSET MANAGEMENT FIRMS WITH MORE THAN $1 TRILLION IN EARLY 2017

Name	Country	Assets under Management (AUM) in Trillions of Dollars
1. BlackRock	US	$5.4
2. Vanguard Group	US	$4.4
3. JPMorgan Chase	US	$3.8
4. Allianz SE (PIMCO)	Germany (US)	$3.3
5. UBS	Switzerland	$2.8
6. Bank of America Merrill Lynch	US	$2.5
7. Barclays Capital	UK	$2.5
8. State Street Global	US	$2.4
9. Fidelity Investments	US	$2.1
10. Bank of New York Mellon	US	$1.7
11. AXA Group	France	$1.5
12. Capital Group	US	$1.4
13. Goldman Sachs Group	US	$1.4
14. Credit Suisse	Switzerland	$1.3
15. Prudential Financial	US	$1.3
16. Morgan Stanley	US	$1.3
17. Amundi[2]	France	$1.1
Total 17 firms (199 Directors)		$41.1 trillion

1. Bob McGlincy, "How Big Is One Trillion Dollars?" *Exhibit City News*, March 2, 2021.
2. Amundi, one of the leading European asset management firms, is a subsidiary of the Crédit Agricole Group.

Additionally, we identified by name, with short biographies, the 199 people who sat on the boards of directors of these seventeen giant firms. The biographies revealed the shared interests and backgrounds of these 199 people.

The term *Giants* referred to the specific firms that controlled up to $5 trillion in capital in 2017. My effort was to identify the most important networks of the global power elite and the individuals therein. I named some 389 individuals in the 2018 book as the core of the policy-planning, nongovernmental networks that manage, facilitate, and protect the continued concentration of global capital. This naming included the 199 mostly white males who served as directors of the seventeen Giants. Additionally, we included the names and biographies of 190 global policy elites who were key decision-makers, operating in support of concentrated global capital in various nongovernmental elite policy organizations including the World Bank, International Monetary Fund, the Group of Thirty, the Group of Twenty, the Group of Seven, the World Trade Organization, the World Economic Forum, the Atlantic Council, the Trilateral Commission, the Bilderberg Group, and the Bank for International Settlements.

In 2017, the top asset management firms were widely invested in each other, making their network a solid core of interlinked companies with shared investments worldwide. For example, JPMorgan Chase and fourteen other trillion-dollar Giants were invested directly in BlackRock, the largest capital management company in 2017 and still the largest in 2023. In 2017, the seventeen Giants collectively invested $403.4 billion in each other. The result of this cross-investment is an interlocked global capital structure that amasses greater and greater wealth in the hands of very few, to the continuing detriment of billions of people worldwide.

Global inequality is never accidental; rather, it's a deliberate circumstance encouraged, maintained, and controlled by global elites via capital investment decisions and policy organizations funded primarily by private capital. Many elites on the boards of directors analyzed in *Giants* may be somewhat unaware of the negative consequences of their decisions, as they primarily focus on seeking higher rates of return on capital. Whether they are cognizant or not, their decisions produce inequality, accelerate environmental devastation, and threaten world peace. I think they have a responsibility to do no harm, and this book is meant to provide them with the knowledge to question the consequences of their decisions. Whether intentional or not, this lack of concern for human betterment is the true crisis of capitalism and the core contradiction of the transnational capitalist class.

In addition to identifying the individuals serving on the boards of the global policy organizations, in *Giants* I examined the role of the protectors of capital, including the US military, which maintains more than eight hundred bases around the world, and an expanding NATO, not to mention numerous intelligence agencies and private military companies. All operate in service to the Giants and the interests of global power elites.

In 2018 I also examined the role of the ideologists serving the media and propaganda needs of the Giants. I showed direct investment by the Giants in all the largest media and news groups, not to mention the world's most influential public relations and propaganda firms (PRP). These news groups and PRP firms cater to the interests of global capital, managing news content, advertising, and other media to maintain an agenda of pro–private capital while serving as an alarm system for any political movements that threaten to restrict freedom of capital investments and profit-making worldwide. PRP firms and the major corporate media know that the core agenda for the global wealth empire and the power elite is the protection of capital growth, insurance of debt collection, and the elimination of barriers and restrictions to the free movement of capital. PRP firms and the transnational media play a vital role in the continuation of the global power elites' capitalist empire. The transnational media and the PRP industry are highly concentrated and fully global. Their primary goal is the promotion of capital growth through the hegemonic, psychological control of desires, emotions, beliefs, and values. PRP firms do this by manipulating the feelings and cognitions of human beings worldwide.

As mentioned above, the term *Giants* refers to the seventeen corporate entities that are global capital management companies with over $1 trillion in assets under management in 2017. By the sociological definition I use, the *Titans* in this book's title refers to the individuals who serve on the boards of directors of the largest capital management companies in the world in 2022. There are now thirty-one Giants—that is, capital asset management companies that manage more than $1 trillion in assets. *Titans of Capital* examines the top ten of those capital management companies in 2022.

In *Titans of Capital*, I present a network analysis that shows how transnational elites interact as a class of people and function as managers of global capital. I identify 117 Titans as a tight network of individuals who are the central managers of concentrated wealth, the facilitators of capital growth, and the primary beneficiaries served by capitalism's protectors: governments, intelligence agencies, military, legal systems, and the corporate media.

The Titans are at the power elite core of the transnational capitalist class. They represent the interests of several hundred thousand millionaires and billionaires who comprise the richest people in the top .05 percent of the world's wealth hierarchy.

The Titans generally know or know of each other—often personally. They do business together, all hold significant personal wealth, share similar educational and lifestyle backgrounds, and retain common global interests. They serve on the boards of directors of the largest major capital investment firms and often other major corporations as well. They meet in nongovernmental policy organizations and form new ones as needs arise to privately make decisions for governments, security forces, and world institutions to implement. The Titans of Capital share a common ideological identity as the engineers of global capitalism, and they hold a mistaken belief that their way of life and the continuous growth of capital are best for all humankind.

I also address critiques made by readers of my 2018 book, *Giants*. One critique of *Giants* was that having 389 people named in the book was too large a number to effectively evaluate. By using the top ten asset management companies in the world today, this new analysis focuses on 117 Titans, a number easier to evaluate and understand. Notably, the 117 directors in 2022 control more investment capital than all 199 directors did in 2017.

Titans of Capital also addresses the consequences of investments by the Titans that negatively impact billions of people around the world. Harmful investments threaten human existence and suspend democratic decision-making on the uses of global resources.

Some readers wanted *Giants* to address the roles of China

and Russia in the constitution of the global power elite. How do capital assets held in these two nations fit into an analysis of concentrated global capital? To address these concerns, I completed chapters on Russia and China that address Titan investments in both countries and the resulting tensions manifested by the war in Ukraine and China's concerns over Taiwan. In *Titans of Capital*, I examine how wars and the threat of war are very profitable for the Titans and their accumulation of capital.

In Chapter 1, I review the massive consolidation of capital wealth management that has occurred in the past five years. The number of trillion and multitrillion dollar capital investment management companies (Giants) has nearly doubled from seventeen in 2017 to thirty-one in 2022. These firms hold the core of global capital wealth, with the top ten now managing $50 trillion in combined assets. The Titans are the directors of the top ten capital investment firms who are responsible for investment decisions. The Titans hold the center of global capital in their hands. Governments, military, intelligence agencies, policy groups, corporate media, and other capitalists consider the Titans' concentrated wealth to be a primary interest that requires constant sociopolitical protection and support.

These power relationships—the basic socioeconomic structure of capitalism—drive the increasingly severe inequalities that relegate millions of people to brutal lives of extreme poverty.

Chapter 2 documents the 89 percent increase in wealth holdings by the top ten capital investment companies over the past five years. These top ten investment management companies are led by the 117 people (Titans) on their boards of directors, who I individually identify with biographies featuring stock holdings, net worth from public sources, education, and prior positions. Following that is a sociological analysis of the 117 Titans as a whole, showing net wealth, ethnicity, gender, other corporate boards, country of origin, policy groups, trusteeships, and political donations. I document Titan participation in the top elite private policy councils in the US, including the Council on Foreign Relations, the Business Council, and the Business Roundtable. I also identify key Titan links to the Central Intelligence Agency. A socioeconomic profile of a typical Titan is offered as a final summary analysis.

Chapter 3 examines the Titans' involvement with the World Economic Forum and their recognition of the major crises of capitalism, including environmental destruction, climate change, threats of war, and global inequality. The WEF promotes a "better capitalism" that seeks to address the polycrises of capitalism through conscience-based management called "stakeholder capitalism," whereby corporations engage in profit-making and wealth consolidation with some aspects of human betterment—including environmental, social, and governance (ESG) criteria—in mind. The goal of WEF stakeholder capitalism is to continue capital growth and economic wealth concentration while using the WEF and ESG criteria as international mechanisms to mediate environmental and socioeconomic threats.

Chapter 4 addresses the idea of socially harmful investments made by the Titans, who maintain massive stakeholdings in tobacco, alcohol, plastics, firearms, gambling, and private prisons. Investments of this kind foster physical addictions, health difficulties, violent shootings, and environmental pollution, affecting billions of people around the world.

Chapter 5 reviews Titan investments in war industries and the international weapons trade. The research includes Titan investments in the top ten Western arms manufacturers. Additionally, I look at how the United States and NATO support permanent war and war profiteering around the world. Also covered are Titan investments in the nuclear weapons industry—despite the Treaty on the Prohibition of Nuclear Weapons, signed by ninety-two nations.

Chapter 6 addresses the rapid advancement of economic growth in China, which is now outproducing the United States. Included is China's development of a widespread middle class and the elimination of extreme poverty (defined as individuals living on less than $2.15 per day). The Titans have widespread investments in China. China is emerging as a direct challenger to US predominance in world trade and is becoming the center of multipolar economic power through the BRICS alliance of Brazil, Russia, India, China, and South Africa. The United States is challenging China using a number of tactics, including economic restrictions, military encirclement, and the expanded arming of Taiwan.

Chapter 7 considers continuing competition between Russia and the US–NATO alliance. I discuss how the US-engineered regime change in Ukraine, in 2014, threatened Russia's Black Sea naval ports. The possible loss of Crimea and attacks on ethnic Russians in Ukraine led Russia to engage in a limited war in Ukraine that has been widely condemned by Western allies. The Titans held widespread investments in Russia, some of which have lost value or are restricted by Russian and US governmental controls. The goal of the US and NATO is a political change in Russia and the reopening of investment opportunities for the Titans.

Chapter 8 examines the links between global inequality, environmental threats, and continued concentration of Titan wealth. A planetary crisis is amplified by unrestricted global wealth concentration and continued massive profit-taking by the Titans and other capital wealth holders. The effort by the US and NATO to build a Joint All-Domain Command and Control system is nothing less than a technological attempt to dominate the world with military might in support of Titan private wealth. Our responsibility as humanitarian global citizens is to build grassroots democratic structures that openly challenge wealth concentration and the Titans' control of world resources.

I concluded *Giants* with a letter to the global elites it analyzed, reminding them of the importance of the Universal Declaration of Human Rights, which the United Nations ratified in 1948. The letter was signed by ninety-one associates and friends, including academics, spiritual leaders, environmentalists, and political and social justice activists. The text of this letter—included as an appendix—remains true. It should be read and considered by the 117 Titans who manage the world's wealth today.

CHAPTER 1

TITANS OF CAPITAL
Concentrated Global Elites Manage World Wealth

The transnational capitalist class manages the world's wealth and makes decisions on capital investment strategies that benefit its collective interests. In fiscal year 2022–23, close to $50 trillion of investment capital was controlled by only ten multitrillion-dollar capital investment management firms, which in turn are managed by 117 Titans on their boards of directors.

The concept of Titans comes from a family of gods in Greek mythology. *Merriam-Webster* defines a titan as "one that is gigantic in size or power: one that stands out for greatness of achievement." Under capitalism, privately held wealth is admired and protected by governmental institutions, intelligence agencies, and military power as a vital interest of the empire. I believe that it is very fitting to apply the concept of Titans to those at the center of global capital accumulation.

Private capital investments serve as the primary operating funds for international arms sales, war-making, and other socially negative activities. These investments fuel the continued use of carbon-based energy, leading to an amplified global climate crisis. Additionally, Titan-managed private funds are invested in tobacco, alcohol, plastics, firearms, gambling, and private prisons, all of which to some extent have impacts on social and mental health and general life expectancy.

In addition to the side effects of negative social investments, one of the Titan's ongoing problems is the need for expanded investment opportunities for ongoing profit returns on investment. Essentially, these firms are locked into a global system that requires continued growth. The resulting concentration of capital threatens human survival and limits the options for reform and corrective action.

Using data from 2017, *Giants: The Global Power Elite* identified seventeen investment management companies that collectively controlled $41.1 trillion. Five years later there were thirty-three investment companies with assets under management (AUM) of more than $1 trillion each.[1] In 2022, these thirty-three giants controlled a collective AUM of $83.12 trillion. The numbers demonstrate rapid growth in consolidated wealth management within Western capitalist countries. Seven of the top ten asset management firms are headquartered in the United States, including BlackRock, Vanguard, Fidelity Investments, Morgan Stanley, JPMorgan Chase, and Capital Group. These seven firms are joined by Union Bank of Switzerland Group; Amundi, a subsidiary of Crédit Agricole, centered in France; and Allianz/PIMCO, in Germany, which round out the world's ten largest asset management firms. Collectively, these ten firms controlled $49.45 trillion in 2022.

Power elites in support of capital investment are embedded in a system of mandatory growth. Failure for capital to achieve continuing expansion leads to economic stagnation, which can result in depressions, bank failures, currency collapses, and mass unemployment. Many believe that capitalism is an economic system that

---

1. "World's Top Asset Management Firms," ADV Ratings, accessed August 24, 2023.

inevitably adjusts itself via contractions, recessions, and depressions.[1] Power elites are entrapped in a web of enforced growth that requires ongoing global management and the formation of new and ever-expanding capital investment opportunities. This forced expansion becomes a worldwide manifest destiny that seeks total capital domination of all regions of the world.

THE TRANSNATIONAL CAPITALIST CLASS: A REVIEW OF POWER ELITE RESEARCH

A long tradition of sociological research documents the existence of a dominant ruling class in the United States. These elites set policy and determine national political priorities. The American ruling class is complex and competitive. It perpetuates itself through the interaction of families of high social standing with similar lifestyles and corporate affiliations and admittance to the same elite social clubs, private schools, and universities.[2]

The American ruling class, it has long been said, is mostly self-perpetuating,[3] maintaining its influence through policymaking institutions such as the National Association of Manufacturers, the US Chamber of Commerce, the Busi-

1. John Maynard Keynes, "A Self-Adjusting Economic System," *Nebraska Journal of Economics and Business* 2, no. 2 (Autumn 1963): 11–15.
2. See G. William Domhoff, *Who Rules America? The Triumph of the Corporate Rich*, 7th ed. (New York: McGraw Hill, 2014); and Peter Phillips, "A Relative Advantage: Sociology of the San Francisco Bohemian Club" (PhD diss., University of California, Davis, 1994).
3. Early studies by Charles A. Beard, published as *An Economic Interpretation of the Constitution of the United States* (1913), established that economic elites formulated the US Constitution to serve their own special interests. Henry H. Klein, in a 1921 book titled *Dynastic America and Those Who Own It*, argued that wealth in America had power never before known in the world and was centered in the top 2 percent of the population, which owned some 60 percent of the country. In 1937, Ferdinand Lundberg published *America's Sixty Families*, which documented intermarrying, self-perpetuating families for whom wealth was the "indispensable handmaiden of government." In 1945, C. Wright Mills determined that nine out of ten business elites from 1750 to 1879 came from well-to-do families, see Mills, "The American Business Elite: A Collective Portrait," *The Journal of Economic History* 5, suppl. 1 (December 1945).

ness Council, Business Roundtable, the Conference Board, American Enterprise Institute for Public Policy Research, the Council on Foreign Relations, and other business-centered policy groups.[1] These associations have long dominated policy decisions within the US government.

In his 1956 book, *The Power Elite*, C. Wright Mills documented how World War II solidified a trinity of power in the United States, composed of corporate, military, and government elites in a centralized power structure and motivated by class interests and working in unison through "higher circles" of contact and agreement. Mills described how the power elite were those "who decide whatever is decided of major consequence."[2] These higher-circle decision-makers tended to be more concerned with interorganizational relationships and the functioning of the economy as a whole rather than simply advancing their particular corporate interests.[3] Mills is careful to observe that the conception of a power elite does not rest solely on personal friendship but rather a broader ideology of shared goals within the corporate system.[4]

As a segment of the American upper class, these higher-circle policy elites are society's principal decision-makers. Although these elites display some sense of "we-ness," they also tend to have continuing disagreements on specific policies and nec-

---

1. See Robert A. Brady, *Business as a System of Power* (New York: Columbia University Press, 1943); and Val Burris, "Elite Policy-Planning Networks in the United States," in *Research in Politics and Society*, 4th ed., eds. Gwen Moore and J. Allen Whitt (Greenwich, Connecticut: JAI Press, 1992), 111–34.

2. C. Wright Mills, *The Power Elite* (New York: Oxford University Press, 1956), 20.

3. See Michael Soref, "Social Class and Division of Labor within the Corporate Elite," *Sociological Quarterly* 17, no. 3 (June 1976); and two works by Michael Useem: "The Social Organization of the American Business Elite and Participation of Corporation Directors in the Governance of American Institutions," *American Sociological Review* 44, no 4 (Aug. 1979), and *The Inner Circle* (New York: Oxford University Press, 1984).

4. Mills, *The Power Elite*, 284.

essary actions in various sociopolitical circumstances.[1] These disagreements can block aggressive reactionary responses to social movements and civil unrest, as in the case of the labor movement in the 1930s and the civil rights movement in the 1960s. During these two periods, the more liberal elements of policy elites tended to dominate the decision-making process and resulted in the passing of the National Labor Relations and Social Security acts in 1935, as well as the Civil Rights and Economic Opportunity acts in 1964. These pieces of national legislation, seen as concessions to the ongoing social movements and civil unrest, were implemented instead of instituting more repressive policies.

In the past few decades, and especially since the events of 9/11, policy elites in the United States have been mostly united in support of an American empire of military power that maintains a brutal war against resisting groups, typically labeled "terrorists," around the world. This "War on Terror" is more about protecting transnational globalization—the worldwide flow of financial capital, dollar hegemony, and access to oil—than it is quelling terrorism. The United States has a long history of interventions around the globe for the purpose of protecting what it calls "national interests." Increasingly, the North Atlantic Treaty Organization (NATO) serves as an arm of US foreign policy, reflecting both the United States' agenda of global dominance and the broadening, transnational economic nature of US interests.[2]

Capitalist power elites exist around the world. The globalization of trade and capital brings the world's elites into

---

1. Thomas Koenig and Robert Gogel, "Interlocking Corporate Directorships as a Social Network," *American Journal of Economics and Sociology* 40, no. 1 (1981); and Peter Phillips, "The 1934–35 Red Threat and the Passage of the National Labor Relations Act," *Critical Sociology* 20, no. 2 (July 1994).
2. For a discussion of principal figures within the global elite who pursue US military domination of the world as their key agenda, see Peter Phillips, Bridget Thornton, and Celeste Vogler, "The Global Dominance Group: 9/11 Pre-Warnings & Election Irregularities in Context," Project Censored, May 2, 2010.

increasingly interconnected relationships—to the point that scholars, over the past few decades, have begun to theorize the development of a transnational capitalist class (TCC).

In *The Transnational Capitalist Class* (2001), one of the early works on the TCC, Leslie Sklair argued that globalization elevated transnational corporations to more influential international roles, with the result that nation-states became less significant than international agreements developed through the World Trade Organization and other international institutions.[1] Emerging from these multinational corporations are members of a transnational capitalist class, whose loyalties and interests, while still rooted in their corporations, are increasingly international in scope.[2]

Sklair wrote that "a new class is emerging that pursues people and resources all over the world in its insatiable desire for private profit and eternal accumulation. This new class is the transnational capitalist class (TCC), composed of corporate executives, globalizing bureaucrats and politicians, globalizing professionals, and consumerist elites."[3] Sklair explained how the TCC functions as an emerging control mechanism of globalization, displaying class-like solidarity in its actions. This united class action reproduces itself through a shared belief that continued growth through profit-driven consumerism will, by itself, eventually solve the problems of global poverty, mass inequality, and environmental collapse.[4]

William I. Robinson, a professor at the University of California, Santa Barbara, followed in 2004 with his book *A Theory of Global Capitalism: Production, Class, and State in a Trans-*

1. Leslie Sklair, *The Transnational Capitalist Class* (Oxford, UK: Blackwell, 2001).
2. Portions of this literature review are republished from Peter Phillips, *Giants: The Global Power Elite* (New York: Seven Stories Press, 2018).
3. Sklair, *Transnational Capitalist*, 4.
4. Phillips, *Giants*, 4–7.

national World.[1] Robinson claimed that five hundred years of capitalism had led to a global epochal shift in which all human activity is transformed into capital. In this view, the world had become a single market wherein members of the TCC had increasingly similar lifestyles, patterns of higher education, and consumption habits. The global circulation of capital is at the core of an international bourgeoisie, who operate in oligopolistic clusters around the world. These clusters of elites form strategic transnational alliances through mergers and acquisitions with the goal of increased concentration of wealth and capital. The process of pursuing increasingly concentrated wealth creates an interlocked core of ruling elites.

The concentration of wealth and power at this level tends to overaccumulate in the hands of increasingly fewer elites to the point where capital has limited safe investment opportunities, leading to pressures for speculative or risky investments. Robinson claimed that, within this system, nation-states become little more than population containment zones, and the real decision-making power lies with those who control global capital.[2]

Another important study of the TCC is William K. Carroll's *The Making of a Transnational Capitalist Class* (2010). Carroll's work focused on the consolidation of transnational corporate-policy networks between 1996 and 2006. He used a database of the boards of directors of the five hundred largest global corporations to show the concentrated connections among them and the decreasing number of people involved. According to the data, the average size of corporate boards dropped from twenty members, in 1996, to fourteen, in 2006. Carroll argued that the TCC at the

---

1. William I. Robinson, *A Theory of Global Capitalism: Production, Class, and State in a Transnational World* (Baltimore: John Hopkins University Press, 2004).
2. Robinson, *Theory of Global Capitalism*, 155–6.

centers of these networks benefit from extensive ties to each other, thus providing both the structural capacity and class consciousness necessary for effective political solidarity.[1]

Deeper inside the transnational capitalist class is what David Rothkopf calls the "superclass." In his 2008 book, *Superclass: The Global Power Elite and the World They Are Making*, Rothkopf argued that the superclass constitutes six thousand to seven thousand people, or 0.0001 percent of the world's population.[2] They are the Davos-attending, Gulfstream- or private jet–flying, megacorporation-interlocked, policy-building elites of the world—people at the absolute peak of the global power pyramid. They are 94 percent male, predominantly white, and mostly from North America or Europe. Rothkopf claims that these are the people setting the agendas at the G8 (now the G7 after the exclusion of Russia) and G20 summits, or through NATO, the World Bank, and the WTO. They represent the highest levels of finance capital, transnational corporations, the government, the military, the academy, nongovernmental organizations, spiritual leaders, and even shadow elites. (Shadow elites include, for instance, the deep politics of national security organizations in connection with international drug cartels, who extract eight thousand tons of opium from US war zones annually, then launder $500 billion through transnational banks, half of which are US-based.)[3]

Robinson's book *Global Capitalism and the Crisis of Humanity*

1. William K. Carroll, *The Making of a Transnational Capitalist Class: Corporate Power in the 21st Century* (London and New York: Zed Books, 2010).

2. David Rothkopf, *Superclass: The Global Power Elite and the World They Are Making* (New York: Farrar, Straus and Giroux, 2008).

3. Peter Dale Scott, *American War Machine: Deep Politics, the CIA Global Drug Connection, and the Road to Afghanistan* (Lanham, MD: Rowman & Littlefield Publishers, 2010). See also Alysha Klein and James F. Tracy, "Wachovia Bank Laundered Money for Latin American Drug Cartels," story #22 in *Censored 2013: Dispatches from the Media Revolution*, eds. Mickey Huff and Andy Lee Roth (New York: Seven Stories Press, 2012), 66–68. Accessible online in Project Censored's archive of its annual Top 25 story lists.

(2014) helps frame this section of our first chapter.[1] Robinson claims that the world faces an unprecedented crisis in social inequality, environmental degradation, global violence, and economic destabilization. He says the world system has centralized and over-valued capital to the point that investment opportunities are limited, and there are essentially only three mechanisms for investing excess capital: risky financial speculation, wars and preparation for war, and the privatization of public institutions. The use of these mechanisms tends to undermine the legitimacy of national governments and can lead to the rise of militarized police states to protect capital around the world.

Robinson writes about the fateful division of humanity into three separate groups, the 1 percent, the 20 percent, and the 80 percent, with wealth becoming increasingly concentrated in the upper fifth of the world's population.[2] TCC elites take pride in pointing out that the world has the largest middle class ever.[3] However, that standard of living does not extend to the vast majority of humanity and likely never will under global capitalism as it is organized in the world today.

Robinson's most recent books, *Global Civil War: Capitalism Post-Pandemic* (2022) and *Can Global Capitalism Endure?* (2022), highlight the massive global suffering and social unrest accelerated by the COVID-19 virus and increased authoritarian controls by governments across the globe. For example, Robinson describes how there were more than 130,000 homeless people in Los Angeles in 2020, 1,000 of whom died in the streets in the first ten months of that year. This homelessness

---

1. Robinson, *Global Capitalism and the Crisis of Humanity*.
2. William I. Robinson, "Global Capitalism and the Restructuring of Education: The Transnational Capitalist Class' Quest to Suppress Critical Thinking," *Social Justice* 43, no. 3 (2016).
3. Rakesh Kochhar, "Are You in the Global Middle Class? Find Out with Our Income Calculator," Pew Research Center, July 21, 2021.

was not due to a lack of housing; there were some 93,000 vacant units in Los Angeles at the time. But the people who needed housing could not afford the rent costs. These housing units and more than twenty-two square miles of vacant lots were mostly owned by corporate developers and multinational investment funds seeking speculative returns on their unoccupied holdings. While thousands suffered, the TCC elites capitalized on unused housing and land.

Los Angeles's inequality problem is amplified worldwide. After the recession of 2008 the Federal Reserve provided $16 trillion in bailouts to banks and corporations around the world.[1] These funds allowed for an even greater concentration of capital among the global .05 percent and led to widespread speculative investing in commodities, land, and cryptocurrencies.

Robinson describes how bailout capital is fictitious money that is no longer based on commodities or production. Whereas in 2018 the gross world product (the total value of goods and services) was some $75 trillion, the speculative derivative market (futures and options) was estimated at $1.2 quadrillion.[2] As a result, wealth concentration is based on speculative investment returns using a growing concentration of fictitious capital controlled by an increasingly small number of people among the global elite .05 percent. In 2020 the COVID-19 pandemic pushed the global economy into free fall, spurring many governments to provide massive bailouts for capital. The US and the European Union provided some $8 trillion in handouts to private corporations in the first few months of the pandemic.

In *Can Global Capitalism Endure?* Robinson concludes

---

1. Robinson, "Restructuring of Education," 20.
2. William I. Robinson, *Global Civil War: Capitalism Post-Pandemic* (Oakland, CA: PM Press, 2022), 21.

that civil unrest, class resistance to wealth concentration, and increasing inequality inevitably produce warlike tensions between the TCC .05 percent and the billions of humans with minimal wealth or financial opportunity. Robinson writes, "If humanity is to survive, global capitalism must ultimately be overthrown and replaced by an ecosocialism."[1] The term *ecosocialism* refers to a democratic, grassroots decision-making process that uses global capital to benefit human rights while sustainably protecting the world's environment.

The most important issue for the TCC/power elite and the Titans of Capital is protecting capital investment. If defending the environment is profitable, then green investments are acceptable. What remains unacceptable is investing in people, the environment, or services that do not benefit capitalism.

To summarize: Wealth concentration by .05 percent of the world's population is managed by an increasingly tighter network of capital investment companies. There are 117 superconnected asset directors on the boards of the top ten asset management firms—each with trillions of dollars in assets under management—representing the financial core of the world's transnational capitalist class in 2022. They directly controlled close to $50 trillion of capital in fiscal year 2022–2023.

Additionally, in 2022 thirty-three capital investment firms, now Giants, managed more than $1 trillion each. This is close to doubling the number of trillion-dollar companies since 2017.[2]

---

1. William I. Robinson, *Can Global Capitalism Endure?* (Atlanta, GA: Clarity Press, 2022), 86.
2. Additional firms with AUM over $1 trillion include: Goldman Sachs, US, $2.39T; Bank of New York Mellon, US, $2.2T; Legal & General, UK, $1.8T; Edward Jones, US, $1.7T; Prudential Financial, US, $1.62T; Deutsche Bank, Germany, $1.6T; Bank of America, US, $1.57T; Invesco, US, $1.5T; T. Rowe Price, US, $1.55T; Northern Trust, US, $1.48T; Franklin Resources, US, $1.47T; Wellington Management, US, $1.42T; BNP Paribas, France, $1.38T; TIAA, US, $1.37T; Natixis Investment Managers, France, $1.3T; AXA, France, $1.1T; HSBC Holdings, UK, $1.19T; Aegon, Netherlands, $1.09T; Sun Life Financial, Canada, $1.08T; Insight Investment, UK, $1.07T; Ameriprise Financial, US, $1.1T.

Continued concentration of global capital increases inequality, starvation, and civil unrest and threatens the lives of millions of people living in extreme poverty. A potential human extinction crisis involving war, climate change, and mass health issues is driven by capitalism's exceedingly concentrated wealth and inability or unwillingness to make necessary adjustments to protect humankind. Extreme wealth creates greater inequality in the world and threatens human existence.

EXTREME WEALTH INCREASING ALONG WITH EXTREME POVERTY

The world's richest 1 percent have "grabbed nearly two-thirds of all new wealth created since 2020," Oxfam America's director of economic justice, Nabil Ahmed, told Voice of America in January 2023.[1] The number of individuals with a net worth of $50 million or more has increased by 50.3 percent in the last decade, and billionaire wealth has grown by 100.3 percent, representing a gain of $5.9 trillion.[2] In the first six months of 2023, the world's richest people on the Bloomberg Billionaires Index added a total of $852 billion to their fortunes.[3]

There are 1.4 million people in the US with a net wealth of more than $5 million, and their combined wealth is greater than $28 trillion. The wealth of the top 10 percent of the United States' richest people makes up 69.7 percent of the country's household wealth and represents 31.5 percent of the

1. Henry Ridgwell, "Oxfam: World's Richest 1% 'Grab Two-Thirds of Global Wealth,'" Voice of America, January 16, 2023.
2. Chuck Collins and Omar Ocampo, "Report: 'Extreme Wealth: The Growing Number of People with Extreme Wealth and What an Annual Wealth Tax Could Raise,'" Institute for Policy Studies, January 17, 2023.
3. Jerry White, "World's Richest Added $852 Billion to Their Fortunes in First Half of 2023," World Socialist Web Site, July 3, 2023.

world's household wealth. In her foreword to Oxfam's 2022 report *Inequality Kills*, Disney heiress Abigail Disney wrote, "There is more than enough money to solve most of the world's problems. It's just being held in the hands of millionaires and billionaires who aren't paying their fair share."[1]

In 2017 the *Los Angeles Times* reported that "1 in 9 people go to bed hungry each night."[2] In 2023, the United Nations World Food Program reported that 258 million people suffer from chronic hunger.[3]

In addition, one in three people in the world suffer from some form of malnutrition, meaning they lack sufficient vitamins and minerals in their diet, which can lead to health issues such as stunted growth in children. Each year, poor nutrition kills 3.1 million children under the age of five.[4] Oxfam calculates that inequality in the world is rapidly increasing, as 1.7 billion workers live in countries where inflation exceeds income. Oxfam's data shows that at least 21,300 people worldwide die daily from inequality, amplified by a lack of both baseline health care and adequate nutrition for billions.[5]

This slaughter is occurring around the world every day. Starvation is mostly the result of people having too little money to purchase food for their families. These families lack resources for acquiring the nutrition needed to keep their children alive and healthy.

Forty-seven percent of the world live on less than $6.85 per day. Extreme poverty—defined as an individual making less than

1. See Nabil Ahmed et al., *Inequality Kills: The Unparalleled Action Needed to Combat Unprecedented Inequality in the Wake of COVID-19* (Oxfam, 2022).

2. Ann M. Simmons, "On World Hunger Day, a Look at Why So Many People Don't Get Enough Food," *Los Angeles Times*, May, 28, 2017.

3. "Global Report on Food Crises: Number of People Facing Acute Hunger Rose to 258 Million in 2022," World Food Program (United Nations), May 8, 2023.

4. Simmons, "On World Hunger Day."

5. Ahmed et al., *Inequality Kills*.

$2.15 per day—was slowly declining during the three decades preceding the pandemic, but this trend was reversed in 2020, after COVID-19 spread.[1] At that point, inequality was amplified as wealth concentration accelerated for the 1 percent and declined for the 99 percent, forcing 180 million more people into extreme poverty. Developing countries, women, and ethnic minorities were hardest hit by the pandemic.[2] The number of people in extreme poverty rose to more than 700 million. According to the World Bank, the rate of global extreme poverty reached 9.3 percent in 2020, up from 8.4 percent in 2019.[3]

Extreme poverty has been amplified by not only the COVID-19 pandemic but also rapidly increasing food prices. Chronic hunger is mostly a problem of distribution, as one-third of all food produced in the world is wasted and lost.[4] The top four global grain companies by revenue in 2022 are:

- Cargill (incorporated in Wilmington, Delaware; based in Minnetonka, Minnesota): $165 billion; and

- Archer-Daniels-Midland (based in Chicago): $85.2 billion;

- Bunge (incorporated in Bermuda; headquarters in St. Louis, Missouri): $67.2 billion;

- Louis Dreyfus Company (headquarters in Rotterdam, Netherlands): $35.5 billion.

In August 2022, the *Guardian* reported that these four companies

---

1. "Poverty," Understanding Poverty, Topics, The World Bank, accessed August 28, 2023.
2. Kate Whiting, "Oxfam: This Is What Inequality Looks Like in 2022—and 6 Ways to Solve It," World Economic Forum, January 17, 2022.
3. "Poverty," The World Bank.
4. Whiting, "What Inequality Looks Like."

control an estimated 70 to 90 percent of the global grain trade.[1] They are making windfall record profits from skyrocketing food prices, which increased by more than 20 percent in 2022. At the same time, 345 million people suffer from acute food insecurity.[2]

The Cargill family privately controls their company, with fourteen family members on the *Forbes* billionaires list.[3]

Major shareholders of Archer-Daniels-Midland from the Titan-controlled top ten capital investment firms include Vanguard ($7.5 billion), Capital Group ($4.5 billion), State Street ($3 billion), and BlackRock ($2.1 billion).

Top Titan shareholders of Bunge are Vanguard ($2.7 billion), Capital Group ($1.8 billion), BlackRock ($811 million), Fidelity Investments FMR ($464 million), State Street ($366 million), and UBS ($205 million).

Louis Dreyfus Company is family owned but recently allowed ADQ, a holding company based in the United Arab Emirates, to invest in a 45 percent share of the company, valued at $800 million.[4]

Readers may tend to assume that food insecurity primarily affects people in lands distant from the United States; however, reports from the US Department of Agriculture indicate that in 2021 some 118 million Americans lived in food-insecure households, with family members skipping meals, eating less, and relying on food banks.[5]

---

1. Fiona Harvey, "Record Profits for Grain Firms amid Food Crisis Prompt Calls for Windfall Tax," *The Guardian*, August 23, 2022.

2. Jessica Corbett, "'Disaster Capitalism at Its Worst': Profits of Grain Giants Spark Global Criticism," Common Dreams, August 23, 2022.

3. Drake Baer, "The Secretive Cargill Family Has 14 Billionaires Thanks to an Agricultural Empire—more than Any Other Clan on Earth," *The State Journal-Register* (Springfield, IL), March 2, 2015.

4. "Louis Dreyfus Company to Enter into Strategic Partnership with ADQ," Louis Dreyfus Company, press release, November 11, 2020.

5. Economic Resource Service, "Food Security in the U.S.," Key Statistics and Graphics, USDA, 2022.

The top three consumer food companies in the United States—General Mills, Kraft Heinz, and Mondelēz International—had combined net earnings for the first quarter of 2023 that were 51 percent higher than in 2022, representing profits of $3.47 billion. The three firms paid $1.3 billion to shareholders for the start of 2023.[1]

Liz Zelnick, director of economic security and corporate power at Accountable.US, stated, "It's shameful that Americans are left food insecure and have to skip meals while corporations and their wealthy shareholders enjoy the spoils of supersized profits under unjustified price hikes."[2] The top investor shareholders in the three largest home food companies in the United States include

- General Mills: Titan investors: Vanguard ($8.3 billion), Capital Group ($5.1 billion), BlackRock ($3.8 billion), and State Street ($2.8 billion);

- Kraft Heinz: Titan Investors: Vanguard ($4.3 billion), BlackRock ($2.2 billion), State Street ($1.7 billion), Capital Group ($980 million), and Fidelity Investments ($330 million); and

- Mondelēz International: Titan Investors: Vanguard ($14.8 billion), State Street ($5.2 billion), BlackRock ($4.8 billion), Fidelity Investments ($2.4 billion), Capital Group ($2.2 billion), and JPMorgan Chase ($1.3 billion).

The US Titans feast on massive food profits as millions of Americans go hungry. Hunger levels in the United States are even higher than in other countries due to increasing food prices

---

1. Harvey, "Grain Firms amid Food Crisis."
2. Jessica Corbett, "Big Food Raking in Huge Profits from Price Hikes as US Hunger Persists: Analysis," Common Dreams, May 10, 2023.

and wealth concentration.[1] There are 2,668 billionaires on 2022 *Forbes* ranking of the planet's richest people. These billionaires are worth a collective $12.7 trillion. The *Forbes* billionaire list, its thirty-sixth annual, reported massive wealth consolidation from 2018 to 2022. More than 1,000 billionaires are much richer than they were four years ago. The United States still leads the world with 735 billionaires, worth a collective $4.7 trillion. China (including Macau and Hong Kong) remains number two with 607 billionaires, worth a collective $2.3 trillion. Nearly four hundred *Forbes* billionaires achieved their holdings primarily through finance and investments, making investment management a significant sector of wealth consolidation.[2]

FOUR-YEAR WEALTH GAINS (2018–2022) FOR BILLIONAIRES WORTH MORE THAN $100B IN 2022

Name, Country	Company	Wealth Gain, 2018–2022
Elon Musk, US	Tesla & SpaceX	$199.9 billion
Bernard Arnault, FR	LVMH (Moët, Hennessy)	$158 billion
Warren Buffett, US	Berkshire Hathaway	$118 billion
Larry Page, US	Alphabet (Google)	$62.2 billion
Sergey Brin, US	Alphabet (Google)	$59.5 billion
Jeff Bezos, US	Amazon	$59 billion
Larry Ellison, US	Oracle	$48 billion
Bill Gates, US	Microsoft	$39 billion[3]

Average four-year gains for these eight billionaires: $92.95 billion

Billionaires are part of a superclass, but not all billionaires are part of the political and policy structures of the power elite that directly influence global decision-making. However, almost all billionaires would agree that protecting their own wealth

---

1. Corbett, "Big Food Raking in Huge Profits."
2. Rob LaFranco et al., "World's Billionaires List: The Richest in 2024," *Forbes*, 2024.
3. Ibid.

and its continued growth is a top priority for nation-states, and using military and law enforcement to do so is acceptable.[1]

A network analysis examining extensive ties among global elites was published by Sandra Navidi in her 2017 book, *Superhubs: How the Financial Elite and Their Networks Rule Our World.* Navidi is the founder and CEO of BeyondGlobal, where she provides macroeconomic and strategic planning to global investment elites. To Navidi, "superhubs" harbor the best-connected, most powerful executives, who by their similar backgrounds, elite education, concentrated wealth, and historical family connections coordinate decision-making networks for concentrations of similar elites. Navidi cites Larry Fink, CEO of BlackRock; Jamie Dimon, CEO of JPMorgan Chase; and global investor and philanthropist George Soros as key individuals at the centers of nodes of interconnected individuals. Their personal relationships are facilitated by the World Economic Forum's annual gathering in Davos, Switzerland, where they host dinners for billionaires and capital investment groups. These superhub elites are mostly wealthy, married white males who travel internationally via private jets and see each other at various financial events and private clubs around the world in places like New York, London, Paris, and Singapore. Navidi acknowledges that financial investments are increasingly concentrated by global elites, which leads to greater inequality in the world that can result in civil unrest and global instability.[2]

As indicated in this chapter, the Titans are the direct capital-management elite, mostly emerging from higher circles of the US capitalist upper class. The Titans now control $50 trillion

---

1. David Rothkopf, "Superclass," Carnegie Endowment for International Peace, April 9, 2008, C-SPAN video, 1:04:19.

2. Sandra Navidi, *Superhubs: How the Financial Elite and Their Networks Rule Our World* (London and Boston: Nicholas Brealey Publishing, 2017).

of concentrated global monetary wealth. The financialization of the world's wealth—concentrated from decades of corporate profits and excess inherited wealth held by the richest people on Earth—now serves as the core of monetary capital around the globe. This wealth is held by the few to the detriment of the billions of people living in hunger and poverty.[1] The recognition of this moral dilemma and the necessary adjustments for humankind are the fundamental messages presented in this book.

SOCIOLOGICAL METHODS STATEMENT

The Titans are an exclusive set of people who control the highest levels of centralized global investment capital. Selecting the top ten capital investment company directors and labeling them Titans gives us specific parameters for evaluating the idea of a capital management system that global elites coordinate and benefit from. Capitalist governments, intelligence agencies, military authorities, policy foundations, and wealthy individuals (millionaires and billionaires) all recognize the Titans and their management of $50 trillion as the prime special interest to which they all hold allegiance. To the world's transnational capitalist class, the Titans represent the importance of centralized capital, consolidated wealth, and systemic growth in their own stations in the hierarchy of global power and wealth.

Selecting the top ten companies should not be taken to mean that other companies are inconsequential. Designation of the top ten companies provides a sociological dataset to focus analysis of a broader system of capitalist wealth inequality, the

---

1. A 2022 World Bank report indicated that, based on data from 2019, "nearly half of the world's population (47 percent) lives in poverty when this is measured as living on less than US$6.85 a day." See World Bank, *Poverty and Shared Prosperity 2022: Correcting Course* (Washington, DC: World Bank, 2022).

destructive consequences of which impact billions of people worldwide.

For example, Goldman Sachs is the eleventh-largest capital management company, with assets under management (AUM) totaling $2.7 trillion, a figure only slightly lower than that of the Capital Group. The Goldman Sachs board of directors is filled with wealthy, high-level corporate officials, many of whom have attended the World Economic Forum and claim to be sensitive to environmental, social, and governance (ESG) factors.[1] Goldman Sachs's directors could easily be counted as Titans, as could the directors of other capital management investment companies. Examining the top ten investment management firms, from within an industry of hundreds, gives us a representative sample of the capital investment system worldwide.

The Titans identified here are a set of real people for whom capitalism provides a unique opportunity to bring havoc—or, possibly, human betterment—to the world. Unfortunately, havoc is currently manifesting more broadly, as the Titans are trapped by the structural demands for continuing growth and profitable returns on the $50 trillion they manage.

I do not believe or claim that any individual Titan is engaged in any *illegal* activities—only that they have *legal* control over enormous amounts of private capital. While acting to fulfill their fiduciary responsibilities to investors, they should also be making decisions that improve the quality of life for all human beings.

---

1. See Chapter 3 for more on the World Economic Forum's promotion of concern for "environmental, social, and governance" (ESG) factors.

CHAPTER 2

WHO CONTROLS WORLD CAPITAL?

The global richest .05 percent represents some 40 million people, including more than 36 million millionaires and 2,600 billionaires, who turn over their excess capital to investment management firms like BlackRock and JPMorgan Chase. The top ten of these firms together controlled close to $50 trillion in 2023. These firms are managed by the 117 people identified below. The top ten capital investment companies extensively cross-invest in each other. Cross-investments between the top ten firms amounted to $320.52 billion in 2022. Cross-investment practices imply a close monitoring of each other's policies and a commonality of mutual interests in market maintenance and growth.

The 117 Titans decide how and where global capital will be invested. Their biggest problem is that they have more capital than there are safe investment opportunities, which can lead to risky speculative investments, increased war spending, privatization of the public domain, and pressures to open new capital investment opportunities through regime change, war, and political manipulations. Ironically, this extreme accumulation of concentrated capital at the top creates a continuing problem for the global money managers, who continually scour and manipulate the world for adequate investment opportunities that will yield profitable capital returns.

THE TOP TEN GLOBAL CAPITAL INVESTMENT COMPANIES
Changes in Assets under Management (AUM) from 2017 to 2022[1]

	AUM in Trillions		
	2017	2022	% Increase
BlackRock (US)	5.4	9.57	77.2
Vanguard Group (US)	2.2	8.1	268
UBS (Switzerland)	2.8	4.38	56.4
Fidelity Investments (US)	2.1	4.5	114.2
State Street (US)	2.4	4.02	67.5
Morgan Stanley (US)	1.3	3.32	155.3
JPMorgan Chase (US)	3.8	2.96	-22.1[2]
Amundi (France)	1.4	5.1	264
Allianz/PIMCO (Germany)	3.3	4.8	45.4
Capital Group (US)	1.4	2.7	92.8
Totals	$26.1	$49.45	89.4%

Each Titan is paid hundreds of thousands of dollars for their board service and receives free or discounted shares of the company's stock, often quickly exceeding millions of dollars in value.

Of the 117 Titans, 86 percent (101) are white, mostly from the US and Europe. Men hold 65 percent of the Titan positions; women hold 35 percent. Sixteen are people of color—one is a Hispanic male, four are Black men, three are Black women, two are Japanese men, one is a US citizen of Chinese descent, one is an Arab male, three are Asian women, and one is South Asian.

It is safe to say that the Titans are very well-off in terms of income and stock holdings. I was able to determine some por-

---

1. Various sources rank assets under management (AUM) values, resulting in slight differences. Our analysis of the top ten is derived from ADV Ratings' data. See "World's Top Asset Management Firms," ADV Ratings, accessed August 29, 2023.

2. Palash Ghosh, "J.P. Morgan AUM Drops 7.3% in Tumultuous Quarter," *Pensions & Investments*, July 14, 2022.

tion of their individual wealth by using their companies' annual Securities and Exchange Commission reports, which are publicly available and list salaries and stock holdings of their boards of directors. Many of the Titans hold more than one directorship position on various company boards. Private companies are not required to list directors' salaries or shareholdings, but that information is often available from annual reports or news articles. In a few cases I had to estimate salaries and holdings based on comparable positions, either in the same company or other organizations. In the data reported below, I clearly state when I am estimating salary or stockholdings.

While it can be determined that there are thousands of people with personal holdings equal to or greater than the individual 117 Titans, what makes them significant is their responsibility for investment decisions on close to $50 trillion. Sitting on the boards at the uppermost concentration of capital wealth in the global investment network, their decisions accelerate capital concentration, impact the environment, earn profits from regional and global wars, undermine democracies, and endanger socioeconomic stability for all.

TITANS' INDIVIDUAL WEALTH HOLDINGS, BASED ON STOCK AND INCOME REPORTS
(n=117)

	Over $1B	Over $100M	Over $10M	Over $5M	Over $1M	Under $1M
Individuals	7	8	26	24	35	17

The wealthiest Titan reportedly holds $60 billion. The seventeen Titans with public holdings of less than $1 million will likely become millionaires in the very near future if they are not already. Again, these numbers represent publicly known figures and almost certainly underestimate each individual's actual worth, because much wealth remains undisclosed or located abroad.

TITANS OF CAPITAL 2022–23
(n=117)

Individuals from 21 countries

United States, 66	56.4 %
France, 17	14.5 %
UK, 5	4.3 %
Germany, 5	4.3 %
Switzerland, 3	2.5 %
Italy, 3	2.5 %
Canada, 3	2.5 %
Japan, 2	1.7 %

One person from each of the following countries: Romania, Austria, Spain, Bulgaria, Singapore, China, Ireland, India, Australia, New Zealand, Sweden, Mexico, Kuwait

Biography Indicators
CB: Current Boards
PE: Prior Employment
PC: Policy Councils
E: Education
F: Financial Wealth

BLACKROCK
Seventeen directors, AUM $9.5 trillion
REVENUE: $17.8 billion (2022)

Titan Cross-Investors in 2022:

Vanguard	$17.4 billion
State Street	$4.3 billion
Capital Group	$4.9 billion
Fidelity Investments	$1.09 billion
Morgan Stanley	$1.4 billion

LAURENCE (LARRY) D. FINK, US
CB: PNC Financial Services Group; Innovir Laboratories (private); CEO, BlackRock **PE**: The First Boston Corporation, VIMRx Pharmaceuticals **PC**: Financial Services Roundtable; Museum of Modern Art; trustee, World Economic Forum (2019); Davos annually, 2019–2023; International Business Council; Business Roundtable; director, Council on Foreign Relations; trustee, New York University **E**: University of California, Los Angeles (MBA, BA) **F**: Net worth $1 billion (2022); BlackRock compensation: $36 million (2021), BlackRock shares: 608,271, value: $428.1 million (2021), sold around 40,960 shares for around $30 million (2022); awarded the title of CEO of the Decade by *Financial News* (2011); donated $50,000-plus to the Council on Foreign Relations (2016); listed by *Forbes* as a new billionaire (2022)[1]

BADER M. ALSAAD, Kuwait
CB: BlackRock; Mercedes-Benz Group AG; chairman of the board and director general, Arab Fund for Economic and Social Development ($12.936 billion) **PC**: Global Advisory Council of Bank of

---

1. "Larry Fink," Billionaires, Profile, *Forbes*, April 4, 2022.

America, Kuwait Fund for Arab Economic Development, supervisory board of Daimler AG, World Economic Forum **PE**: Director and managing director, Kuwait Investment Authority (KIA); chief executive officer, Kuwait Financial Centre; chairman and deputy chairman, International Forum of Sovereign Wealth Funds **E**: Al-Imam Muhammad Ibn Saud Islamic University (MA in economics) **F**: BlackRock compensation: $355,640 (2021); BlackRock shares: 1,201, value: $855,940 (2021), Mercedes-Benz Group AG compensation: $164,833, share value $69,650; Arab Fund for Economic and Social Development: $600,000 (estimate based on prior chair's compensation)

PAMELA DALEY, US
CB: BlackRock, Patheon NV, Secureworks, BP **PE**: Morgan, Lewis & Bockius; General Electric; BG Group **PC**: World Economic Forum, World Wildlife Fund **E**: University of Pennsylvania Carey Law School (JD), Princeton University (BA) **F**: GE annual compensation: $522,000, until 2014; BlackRock compensation: $379,943 (2021), BlackRock shares: 6,178, value: $4.4 million (2021); Secureworks compensation: $231,998 (2022), Secureworks shares: 217,548, value: $1.3 million (2022); BP compensation: $220,000, BP shares: 40,332, value: $269,014

BETH FORD, US
CB: BlackRock; president and CEO, Land O'Lakes; PACCAR; Starbucks **PE**: Executive vice president and head of supply chain, International Flavors & Fragrances; Clearwater Paper Corporation **PC**: Board of directors, Business Roundtable; World Economic Forum **E**: Columbia Business School (MBA), Iowa State University (BBA) **F**: BlackRock compensation: $45,687 (2021), BlackRock shares: 373, value: $265,833 (2021); PACCAR compensation: $285,039 (2022),

PACCAR shares: 33,803, value: $3.3 million (2022); Land O'Lakes compensation: $450,000; Starbucks compensation: $309,000

WILLIAM E. FORD, US

CB: BlackRock; ByteDance (Toutiao); CEO and chairman, General Atlantic; Sierra Space **PE**: IHS Markit, Axel Springer Digital Classifieds, Morgan Stanley, First Republic Bank, Lincoln Center, Royalty Pharma, Tory Burch **PC**: Director, National Committee on US-China Relations; CEO Action for Diversity & Inclusion; advisory council, McKinsey; advisory board, New York State Life Science; World Economic Forum; the Business Council; Center for Strategic and International Studies; Council on Foreign Relations; Global Private Capital Association; Memorial Sloan Kettering Cancer Center; Partnership for New York City; Rockefeller University; Tsinghua University School of Economics and Management **E**: Stanford Graduate School of Business (MBA), Amherst College (BA) **F**: BlackRock compensation: $378,934 (2021), BlackRock shares: 11,915, value: $8.5 million (2021); General Atlantic compensation: $15.8 million (2021); net worth: $2.07 billion[1]

FABRIZIO FREDA, Italy & US

CB: BlackRock; CEO, the Estée Lauder Companies **PE**: Procter & Gamble, Coca-Cola **PC**: World Economic Forum **E**: University of Naples Federico II (BA) **F**: BlackRock compensation: $340,422 (2021), BlackRock shares: 6,628, value: $4.7 million (2021); Estée Lauder compensation: $19.21 million (2022), Estée Lauder shares: 746,838, value: $195 million (2022); sold shares of Estée Lauder for $476 million over fifteen years[2]

1. "William Ford Net Worth," wallmine, last updated July 5, 2023.
2. "Fabrizio Freda Net Worth & Insider Trades," Insider Trades, Benzinga, July 5, 2023.

MURRY S. GERBER, US

CB: BlackRock, Halliburton, United States Steel Corp. **PE:** CEO, EQT Corporation; Shell **PC:** Pennsylvania Business Council; trustee, Augustana College **E:** University of Illinois Urbana-Champaign (MA in geology), Augustana College (BA) **F:** BlackRock compensation: $465,247 (2021), BlackRock shares: 42,025, value: $30 million (2021); sold 7,849 shares of BlackRock for $5.1 million (2022); Halliburton compensation: $438,044 (2021), Halliburton shares: 551,911, value: $14 million (2022); US Steel Corp. compensation: $285,000 (2021), US Steel shares: 204,314, or $5.2 million (2021); net worth: $368 million, as of December 2022[1]

MARGARET (PEGGY) L. JOHNSON, US

CB: BlackRock; CEO, Magic Leap; Live Nation Entertainment **PE:** Vice president of business development, Microsoft Corporation; executive vice president of Qualcomm Technologies Inc.; president of global market development, Live Nation Entertainment **PC:** Adviser, Huntington's Disease Society of America, San Diego chapter; Asia-Pacific Economic Cooperation Business Advisory Council **E:** San Diego State University (BS) **F:** BlackRock compensation: $365,535, BlackRock shares: 2,396, value: $1.7 million; Microsoft compensation: $750,000 (2020), stock holdings: $7 million; Johnson and Saudi Arabia's Public Investment Fund took control of Magic Leap in 2021, salary: $280,000 (Glassdoor)

ROBERT S. KAPITO, US

CB: BlackRock; president, iCruise.com **PE:** Bain & Co. **PC:** World Economic Forum (2023); International Monetary Conference; the Financial Services Roundtable; trustee, University of Pennsylvania **E:** Harvard Business School (MBA), Wharton School of the Univer-

---

1. "Murry Gerber Net Worth," wallmine, last updated August 1, 2023.

sity of Pennsylvania (BA) **F:** BlackRock compensation: $28.7 million (2022), BlackRock shares: 264,268, value: $188 million (2021)

CHERYL MILLS, US
CB: BlackRock; CEO, BlackIvy Group **PE:** Vice president, New York University; chief of staff to Secretary of State Hillary Clinton; deputy counsel to President Bill Clinton; Cendant Corporation; Orion Power; Oxygen Media; Hogan Lovells **PC:** Clinton Foundation, See Forever Foundation/Maya Angelou Public Charter School, World Economic Forum **E:** Stanford Law School (JD), University of Virginia (BA) **F:** BlackRock compensation: $355,247 (2021), BlackRock shares: 4,855, value: $3.4 million (2021)

GORDON M. NIXON, Canada
CB: BlackRock, Bell Canada, Acasta Enterprises **PE:** Royal Bank of Canada, Newmont Mining, Institute of International Finance, International Monetary Conference, Canadian Council of Chief Executives **PC:** World Economic Forum **E:** Queen's University (BA) **F:** BlackRock compensation: $370,709 (2021), BlackRock shares: 3,375, value: $2.4 million (2021); Bell Canada compensation: $460,000 (2021), Bell Canada shares: 153,484, value: $5 million (2021)

KRISTIN PECK, US
CB: BlackRock; CEO, Zoetis **PE:** Executive vice president, Worldwide Business Development and Innovation at Pfizer; member, Pfizer executive leadership team; the Boston Consulting Group; the Prudential Realty Group; the O'Connor Group; JPMorgan Chase, board member, Catalyst; **PC:** Business Roundtable; World Economic Forum; W. Edwards Deming Center for Quality, Productivity, and Competitiveness at Columbia Business School **E:** Columbia Business School (MBA), Georgetown University (BA) **F:** BlackRock

compensation: $45,687 (2021), BlackRock shares: 373, value: $265,833 (2021); Zoetis CEO salary: $1.2 million, Zoetis shares: 9,600, value: $8.2 million (2022)

CHARLES H. ROBBINS, US
CB: BlackRock; CEO, Cisco Systems **PE:** Bay Networks, Ascend Communications **PC:** Atlanta chapter of Business Executives for National Security, the National MS Society of Northern California, World Economic Forum **E:** University of North Carolina at Charlotte (BA) **F:** BlackRock compensation: $340,422 (2021), BlackRock shares: 2,259, value: $1.6 million (2021); Cisco compensation: $29 million (2022), Cisco shares value: $23.4 million (2022)

MARCO ANTONIO SLIM DOMIT, Mexico
CB: BlackRock; CEO, Grupo Financiero Inbursa; Impulsora del Desarrollo y el Empleo en América Latina; Afore Inbursa; Arrendadora Financiera Inbursa; Operadora Inbursa de Sociedades de Inversión; Seguros Inbursa; Sears Roebuck; America Telecom; América Móvil; Carso Global Telecom; US Commercial Corp.; CompUSA; Grupo Carso **PE:** Director, Teléfonos de México **PC:** World Economic Forum **E:** Universidad Anáhuac **F:** BlackRock compensation: $365,169 (2021), BlackRock shares: 6,079, value: $4.3 million (2021); personal net worth greater than $4.1 billion; son of Carlos Slim Helú, whose estimated net worth is $65 billion

HANS E. VESTBERG, Sweden
CB: BlackRock; chairman and CEO, Verizon Communications; co-chair, New Jersey CEO Council **PE:** President and CEO, Ericsson; Swedish Olympic Committee; Hexagon AB **PC:** Chairman, World Economic Forum; UN Foundation; Whitaker Peace & Development Initiative; EDISON Alliance; Leadership Council of the UN

Sustainable Development Solutions Network **E:** Uppsala University (BA) **F:** BlackRock compensation: $82,267 (2021), BlackRock shares: 425, value: $302,893 (2021); Verizon compensation: $20.3 million (2021), Verizon shares: 149,000, value: $15.85 million

SUSAN LYNNE WAGNER, US
CB: Founding partner, BlackRock; director, DSP Mutal Fund; RBB Fund; Bogle Small Cap Growth Fund **PE:** Lehman Brothers **PC:** World Economic Forum **E:** University of Chicago (MBA), Wellesley College (BA) **F:** BlackRock compensation: $720,788 (2021), Black-Rock shares: 429,239, value $306 million (2021)

MARK WILSON, New Zealand
CB: BlackRock; co-chair and CEO, Abacai **PE:** CEO, Aviva plc; CEO, AIA Group Limited; CEO, AXA **PC:** UN Business and Sustainable Development Commission, World Economic Forum **E:** University of Waikato (BA) **F:** BlackRock compensation: $359,261 (2021), BlackRock shares: 2,134, value: $1.5 million (2021); Aviva compensation: $5.2 million (2018); Abacai compensation: $8.091 million

VANGUARD GROUP
Eleven directors, AUM $8.1 trillion
REVENUE: $6.9 billion (2020)

Titan Cross-Investors in 2022:

JPMorgan Chase	$37 billion
BlackRock	$9.6 billion
Morgan Stanley	$9.6 billion
Fidelity Investments	$3.4 billion

MORTIMER (TIM) J. BUCKLEY, US

CB: Vanguard Group **PE:** Various positions at Vanguard Group, New York Federal Reserve Investment Advisory Committee **PC:** The Children's Hospital of Philadelphia, World Economic Forum **E:** Harvard Business School (MBA), Harvard College (BA) **F:** Vanguard compensation: $700,000 (2021)[1]

TARA BUNCH, US

CB: Vanguard Group; global operations management, Airbnb **PE:** VP, AppleCare; Hewlett-Packard **PC:** WEF Partnership for Global LGBTI Equality (PGLE) **E:** Santa Clara University (MBA), University of California, Berkeley (BS) **F:** Airbnb salary: $600,000, Airbnb share value: $238,000; Vanguard compensation: $300,000

EMERSON U. FULLWOOD, US

CB: Vanguard Group **PE:** Xerox, Amerigroup, General Signal, SPX **PC:** Director, North Carolina A&T University's College of Engineering Industry Advisory Group; World Economic Forum; Rochester Institute of Technology; United Way of Rochester; University of Rochester Medical Center; Monroe Community College Foundation; Rochester Urban League; Colgate Rochester Crozer Divinity School **E:** Columbia University (MBA), North Carolina State University (BA) **F:** SPX compensation: $215,000 (2021), SPX share value: $2.2 million (2021); Vanguard compensation: $300,000

F. JOSEPH LOUGHREY, US

CB: Vanguard Group, Hillenbrand, SKF **PE:** Cummins **PC:** National Association of Manufacturers, World Economic Forum, Kellogg Institute for International Studies at the University of Notre Dame, Chicago Council on Global Affairs, Lumina Foundation for Education, Oxfam

---

1. "The Vanguard Group," Companies, Comparably, accessed August 28, 2023.

America **E:** University of Notre Dame (BS) **F:** Hillenbrand compensation: $333,871 (2021), Hillenbrand shares: 103,256, value: $4.3 million (2021); Vanguard compensation: $300,000 (2022)

MARK LOUGHRIDGE, US

CB: Vanguard Group, Dow Chemical Company **PE:** CFO, IBM (retired 2013) **PC:** Council on Chicago Booth, World Economic Forum **E:** University of Chicago (MBA); Stanford University (BS, BE); École Nationale Supérieure de Mécanique et des Microtechniques, France **F:** Dow compensation: $262,474 (2016), Dow shares: 7,574, value: $534,724 (2016); IBM compensation: $775,000 (2013), IBM shares: 88,317, value: $13.2 million (2013); Vanguard compensation: $300,000 (2022)

SCOTT C. MALPASS, US

CB: Vanguard Group; Catholic Investment Services; Vatican Bank Group; manager, University of Notre Dame's $15 billion endowment (retired 2020); partner, Grafton Street Partners (AUM $282,645,000) (2022) **PE:** St. Joseph Capital Corporation, Bank of New York Mellon, Irving Trust Company **PC:** RoundTable Healthcare Partners, the Investment Fund for Foundations, World Economic Forum **E:** University of Notre Dame (MBA, BA) **F:** Vanguard compensation: $300,000 (2022); University of Notre Dame compensation: $4.8 million (2020)

DEANNA MULLIGAN, US

CB: Vanguard Group, DuPont de Nemours, Purposeful **PE:** President/CEO/board chair and executive vice president, Guardian Life; senior vice president, Life & Annuity; New York Life Insurance Company; AXA Equitable; McKinsey; Arch Capital; chair of the board, ACLI; advisory board member, Guild Education **PC:** NewYork-Presbyterian Hospital, World Economic Forum, Partnership for New York City, Chief Executives for Corporate Purpose, member of the Stanford Graduate School of Business Advisory Council, Bruce Museum in Greenwich, Connecticut **E:** Stanford University (MBA), University of Nebraska-Lincoln (BS) **F:** DuPont de Nemours compensation: $261,119 (2021), DuPont de Nemours shares: 3,798, value: $267,872; Vanguard compensation: $300,000

ANDRÉ F. PEROLD, US & South Africa

CB: Vanguard Group; RIT Capital Partners; partner, CIO; High-Vista Strategies (Cayman Islands, AUM $5 billion 2022) **PE:** Rand Merchant Bank; professor of finance and banking, Harvard University **E:** Stanford University (PhD, MS); University of Witwatersrand, Johannesburg (BSc) **F:** RIT Capital Partners compensation: $49,680 (2021); Vanguard compensation: $300,000 (2022)

SARAH BLOOM RASKIN, US

CB: Vanguard Group **PE:** Managing director, Promontory Financial Group; associate, Arnold & Porter; professor of law, Duke University (2021) **PC:** US Treasury (2014–2017); World Economic Forum; banking counsel, US Senate Committee on Banking, Housing, and Urban Affairs; commissioner of financial regulation, State of Maryland; Federal Reserve Bank of New York; Joint Economic Committee of Congress; trustee, Amherst College **E:** Harvard Law School (JD), Amherst College (BA) **F:** Duke University salary: $207,000; Vanguard compensation: $300,000 (2022); assets between her and her husband, Congressman Jamie Raskin: $6.8 million.[1]

---

1. Bill Turque, "Jamie Raskin: The most liberal congressional candidate in a crowd," *Washington Post*, April 5, 2016.

DAVID THOMAS, US

CB: Vanguard Group, DTE Energy **PE:** Professor of business administration, Harvard Business School; former dean, Georgetown University's McDonough School of Business; assistant professor, Wharton School of the University of Pennsylvania **PC:** American Red Cross, Posse Foundation, World Economic Forum **E:** Yale University (PhD, MPhil, BA), Columbia University (MA) **F:** DTE Energy compensation: $286,305, DTE Energy shares: 6,482, value: $774,987; Vanguard compensation: $300,000 (2022)

PETER F. VOLANAKIS, US

CB: Vanguard Group, CCS Holding **PE:** SPX; CEO, Corning **PC:** Overseer, Tuck School of Business at Dartmouth College; World Economic Forum **E:** Dartmouth College (MA, BA) **F:** Vanguard compensation: $300,000 (2022); Corning compensation: $8.7 million (2010); sold 260,000 shares of Corning in 2010 for $4.68 million

MORGAN STANLEY
Fourteen directors, AUM $3.32 trillion
REVENUE: $53.7 billion (2022)

Titan Cross-Investors in 2022:

Vanguard	$17.6 billion
State Street	$10.3 billion
BlackRock	$7.6 billion
Capital Group	$4.3 billion
JPMorgan Chase	$3.9 billion
Fidelity Investments	$2.1 billion

JAMES P. GORMAN, Australia & US

CB: Chairman and CEO, Morgan Stanley **PE:** Merrill Lynch, McKinsey, Phillips Fox & Masel, MSCI, Visa USA **PC:** Federal Reserve

Bank of New York, Institute of International Finance, Partnership for New York City, Metropolitan Museum of Art, Business Council, Council on Foreign Relations, World Economic Forum, Business Roundtable **E:** Columbia University (MBA), University of Melbourne (BA, LLB) **F:** Morgan Stanley compensation: $10.4 million, Morgan Stanley share value: $24.5 million (2022)

ALISTAIR DARLING (DIED, NOVEMBER 30, 2023), UK

CB: Morgan Stanley **PE:** Member, House of Commons; member, House of Lords; chancellor of the Exchequer (Britain's treasury); secretary of state, Department of Trade and Industry; secretary of state, Department for Work and Pensions; secretary of state, Department of Social Security; secretary of state, Department for Transport; secretary of state, Scotland **PC:** World Economic Forum; Standard Life Foundation; Royal Institute of International Affairs; chairman, Better Together campaign in the Scottish referendum **E:** University of Aberdeen (LLB) **F:** Morgan Stanley compensation: $360,000 (2022), Morgan Stanley share value: $2 million (2022)

THOMAS H. GLOCER, US

CB: Morgan Stanley, K2 Intelligence, Publicis Groupe, Merck **PE:** Instinet Group; New York City Investment Fund Manager; CEO, Thomson Reuters; Angelic Ventures **PC:** Atlantic Council; European Business Leaders Council; Partnership for New York City; James Madison Council of the Library of Congress; advisory board of the British-American Business Council; International Business Council of World Economic Forum; director, Council on Foreign Relations; Wall Street Journal CEO Council **E:** Yale Law School (JD), Columbia University (BA) **F:** Morgan Stanley compensation: $410,000 (2022), Morgan Stanley share value: $7.8 million (2022); Merck compensation: $350,000 (2022), Merck shares: 80,578, value:

$8.8 million (2022); Thomson Reuters compensation: $20 million (2001–2008)

ROBERT H. HERZ, UK & US

CB: Morgan Stanley, Workiva, Federal National Mortgage Association (Fannie Mae) **PE:** WebFilings, Coopers & Lybrand, PricewaterhouseCoopers **PC:** Kessler Foundation, World Economic Forum, Financial Accounting Standards Board, International Accounting Standards Board, Public Company Accounting Oversight Board, Accounting Standards Oversight Council of Canada, SASB Foundation **E:** University of Manchester (BA); chartered public accountant, Federal National Mortgage Association **F:** Morgan Stanley compensation: $385,000 (2022), Morgan Stanley share value: $5.3 million (2022); $4.3 million Morgan Stanley stock sold 2021–2023; Fannie Mae compensation: $182,079 (2016); Workiva compensation: $333,125 (2015), Workiva shares: 67,857, value: $68 million (2022)

ERIKA H. JAMES, US

CB: Morgan Stanley; Momentive Global; dean, Wharton School of the University of Pennsylvania **PE:** Goizueta Business School at Emory University, Executive Education at Darden School of Business, University of Virginia Executive Education at Darden School of Business, Institute for Crisis Management **PC:** Momentive Global, World Economic Forum, Graduate Management Admissions Council, Tsinghua University School of Economics and Management, the Indian School of Business, Save the Children, the Philadelphia Orchestra, Wharton School of the University of Pennsylvania **E:** University of Michigan (PhD), Pomona College (BA) **F:** Momentive Global compensation: $166,826 (2022), Momentive Global share value: $162,865 (2022); Morgan Stanley compensation: $345,000 (2023)

HIRONORI KAMEZAWA, Japan

CB: Morgan Stanley; president and group CEO, Mitsubishi UFJ Financial Group; director, MUFG Bank, Ltd. **PC:** World Economic Forum **E:** Graduate School of Mathematical Sciences, University of Tokyo (MA) **F:** Mitsubishi UFJ Financial Group compensation: ¥252 million ($1.9 million) (2022) (Economic Research Institute); investor agreement with Mitsubishi UFJ Financial Group states no compensation for board service with Morgan Stanley

SHELLEY B. LEIBOWITZ, US

CB: Morgan Stanley; Bitsight; Elastic; president, SL Advisory **PE:** E*TRADE; chief information officer, World Bank Group; Morgan Stanley (2009–2012); Greenwich Capital Markets; Barclays Capital; Investment Risk Management; Massachusetts Mutual Life Insurance Company; Endgame **PC:** Director, New York Board of the National Association of Corporate Directors; Council on Foreign Relations; World Economic Forum; Center for Development Economics at Williams College **E:** Williams College (BA) **F:** Morgan Stanley stock value: $386,065 (2022); net worth $4.1 million[1]

STEPHEN J. LUCZO, US

CB: Morgan Stanley; managing partner, Crosspoint Capital Partners (Cayman Islands, AUM $1.6 billion, 2022); AT&T; CEO, Seagate Technology **PE:** Director, Microsoft; Global Technology Group of Bear Stearns **PC:** All Stars Helping Kids, Balance Vector, World Economic Forum **E:** Stanford (MBA, BA) **F:** Morgan Stanley share value: $702,776 (2022); Seagate Tech salary: $1 million (2009); Microsoft shares: 133,500, value: $34 million; AT&T compensation: $360,000 (2022), AT&T shares: 525,475, value: $9.9 million (2021); Crosspoint salary: $415,000

---

1. "Shelley B. Leibowitz," News, Accueil, Business Leaders Biography, Market Screener, accessed August 28, 2023.

JUDITH (JAMI) A. MISCIK, US

CB: Morgan Stanley, In-Q-Tel (CIA technology management foundation), General Motors, Hewlett-Packard **PE:** CEO, Kissinger Associates; EMC; Lehman Brothers; Barclays Bank; CIA (1983–2005); deputy director for intelligence of the CIA (2005–2008) **PC:** Director, Council on Foreign Relations; National Security Council; American Ditchley Foundation; United Nations Association **E:** University of Denver (MA in international studies), Pepperdine University (BA) **F:** Morgan Stanley compensation: $370,000 (2022), Morgan Stanley stock value: $2.5 million (2022); GM compensation: $361,660 (2020), GM shares: 7,876 (2022), value: $283,536

MASATO MIYACHI, Japan

CB: Morgan Stanley; CEO, Global Corporate and Investment Banking of MUFG Bank **PE:** Bank of Tokyo **E:** Waseda University (PhD), Stanford University (MA), University of Tokyo (BA) **F:** Net worth: ¥110,000,000 ($828,469) (2020) (Economic Research Institute); investor agreement with Mitsubishi UFJ Financial Group states no compensation for board service with Morgan Stanley

DENNIS M. NALLY, US

CB: Morgan Stanley, Globality, AmerisourceBergen **PE:** PricewaterhouseCoopers **PC:** US Council for International Business; US Chamber of Commerce; the Business Roundtable; Partnership for New York City; advisory board at Duke Kunshan University; World Economic Forum; trustee, Carnegie Hall Corporation/The Carnegie Hall Society **E:** Western Michigan University (BBA), Columbia University and Penn State University Executive Programs (CPA) **F:** Morgan Stanley compensation: $370,000 (2022), Morgan Stanley shares: 17,279, value: $1,551,886 (2022); AmerisourceBergen compensation: $350,369 (2022), AmerisourceBergen shares: 4,803, value: $768,480

MARY L. SCHAPIRO, US
CB: Morgan Stanley; CVS Health Corporation; special adviser to the founder and chair, Bloomberg; board of the Value Reporting Foundation **PE:** Duke Energy, General Electric, Mondelēz International **PC:** Vice chair for global public policy, Promontory Financial Group; chair, Commodity Futures Trading Commission; chair, US Securities and Exchange Commission; World Economic Forum; Financial Industry Regulatory Authority **E:** George Washington University (JD), Franklin & Marshall College (BA) **F:** Morgan Stanley compensation: $345,000, Morgan Stanley share value: $1.8 million (2022); CVS compensation: $310,000, CVS shares: 22,227, value: $1.6 million

PERRY M. TRAQUINA, US
CB: Morgan Stanley, Allstate **PE:** CEO, Wellington Management Group; eBay **PC:** World Economic Forum; trustee, Brandeis University and Windsor School **E:** Harvard Business School (MBA), London School of Economics (BA), Chartered Financial Analyst **F:** Morgan Stanley compensation: $385,000 (2022), Morgan Stanley shares: 62,329, value: $5.6 million (2022); eBay compensation: $364,250 (2021), eBay share value: $116,301 (2021); Allstate compensation: $297,184 (2022), Allstate shares: 6,955, value: $892,604 (2022)

RAYFORD WILKINS JR., US
CB: Morgan Stanley, Valero Energy **PE:** H&R Block, AT&T, SBC, Southwestern Bell Telephone, Caterpillar **PC:** Tiger Woods Foundation; adviser, McCombs School of Business at the University of Texas at Austin **E:** The University of Texas at Austin (BA in business administration) **F:** Morgan Stanley compensation: $370,000 (2022), Morgan Stanley shares: 33,145, value: $3 million (2022); Caterpillar compensation: $300,096, Caterpillar stock value: $300,096

(2022); Valero Energy compensation: $355,014 (2022), Valero Energy shares: 33,686 (2022), value: $4 million; listed in *Fortune* as one of the "Nation's 50 Most Powerful Black Executives" in 2002

STATE STREET CORPORATION
Thirteen directors, AUM $4.02 trillion
REVENUE: $12.1 billion (2022)

Titan Cross-Investors in 2022:

Vanguard	$5.3 billion
BlackRock	$1.6 billion
Capital Group	$648 million
Fidelity Investments	$356 million

RONALD P. O'HANLEY, US
CB: Chair, State Street; Unum Group **PE:** Asset management and corporate services, Fidelity Investments; BNY Mellon Asset Management **PC:** World Economic Forum (2023); Greater Boston Chamber of Commerce; Federal Advisory Council, Federal Reserve; the Boston Foundation; the Ireland Funds; IYRS School of Technology & Trades; Syracuse University; WBUR (public radio station in Boston) **E:** Harvard Business School (MBA), Syracuse University (BA) **F:** State Street compensation: $14 million (2021); Unum Group compensation: $290,001 (2021); net worth: $25.9 million (2022)[1]

DAME AMELIA C. FAWCETT, US & UK
CB: State Street, Kinnevik **PE:** Morgan Stanley, Guardian Media Group, Sullivan & Cromwell, Pensions First Group **PC:** Hedge Fund Standards Board; Prince of Wales's charitable foundation; London Business School; World Economic Forum; commissioner, US–UK Fulbright Commis-

---

1. "Ronald O'Hanley Net Worth," wallmine, last updated August 17, 2023.

sion **E:** University of Virginia (JD), Wellesley College (BA) **F:** State Street compensation: $435,552 (2021), State Street share value: $3.6 million (2021); Kinnevik compensation: $83,000 (2016); awarded title of Dame Commander of the Most Excellent Order of the British Empire (2010)

MARIE A. CHANDOHA, US

CB: State Street, Macy's **PE:** Investment management, Charles Schwab; managing director, BlackRock; Barclays Global Investors; Montgomery Fixed Income Division; Wells Capital Management; Investment Company Institute; Zoe Financial **PC:** World Economic Forum, California chapter of the Nature Conservancy **E:** Harvard University (BA) **F:** State Street compensation: $345, 412 (2021), State Street share value: $605,338 (2021); Macy's compensation: $1,779,038 (deferred and restricted stock 2022)

DONNALEE (DONNA) DEMAIO, US

CB: State Street, Hiscox (Bermuda, $2.6 billion revenue) **PE:** VP, American International Group; Arch Insurance Group; United Guaranty; CEO, MetLife Bank; PricewaterhouseCoopers **PC:** World Economic Forum **E:** Muhlenberg College (BA) **F:** State Street compensation: $338,000 (2022); Hiscox compensation: $165,603 (2022)

PATRICK DE SAINT-AIGNAN, US & France

CB: State Street, European Kyoto Fund, Allied World Assurance Company Holdings (Bermuda, $5.9 billion securities) **PE:** Morgan Stanley; director, vice chairman, and US managing partner, Deloitte; director, Bank of China (2006–2008); Natixis Corporate & Investment Banking **E:** Harvard University (MBA), École des Hautes Études Commerciales de Paris (BBA) **F:** State Street compensation: $375,818 (2021), State Street common stock value: $2.4 million (2021)

WILLIAM C. FREDA, US

CB: State Street; Guardian Life Insurance Company of America (private); chairman, Hamilton Insurance Group (Bermuda, private) **PE:** Deloitte **PC:** Committee on Capital Markets Regulation, American Institute of Certified Public Accountants' Insurance Companies Committee, International Accounting Standards Committee's Insurance Steering Committee, Economic Club of New York, National Italian American Foundation **E:** Bentley University (BS) **F:** State Street compensation: $395,818 (2021), State Street common stock value: $1.5 million (2021)

SARA MATHEW, US & India

CB: State Street, Carnival, Federal Home Loan Mortgage Corporation (Freddie Mac), Xos, Dropbox **PE:** CEO, Dun & Bradstreet Corporation; NextGen Acquisition Corporation; Campbell Soup Company; Avon Products; Reckitt Benckiser Group; Shire; VP, Procter & Gamble (India-Asia) **PC:** World Economic Forum, American Chamber of Commerce Singapore, United Way Cincinnati **E:** Xavier University (MBA), University of Madras (BS) **F:** State Street compensation: $350,005 (2022), State Street common stock value: $855,932 (2021); Dropbox compensation: $215,790 (2022), Dropbox share value: $151,656 (2022); Freddie Mac compensation: $290,000 (2021); Xos compensation: $422,500 (2022), Xos share value: $343,577 (2022); Carnival share value: $72,532; Reckitt Benckiser Group compensation: $143,524, Reckitt share value: $7,981 (2022)

WILLIAM L. MEANEY, US

CB: State Street; president, CEO, and director, Iron Mountain **PE:** Qantas Airways, Zuellig Group, Swiss International Airlines, South African Airways **PC:** Asia Business Council; World Economic Forum; Massachusetts General Hospital; trustee, Rensselaer

Polytechnic Institute and Carnegie Mellon University **E:** Carnegie Mellon University (MBA), Rensselaer Polytechnic Institute (BS) **F:** State Street compensation: $375,552 (2021), State Street share value: $897,281 (2021); Iron Mountain compensation: $9.25 million (2021)

SEAN O'SULLIVAN, Canada & UK
CB: State Street; managing partner, SOSV (AUM $15 billion) **PE:** HSBC Holdings, HFC Bank **PC:** Information Technology Advisory Committee at the University of British Columbia, York University Foundation **E:** The University of Western Ontario (BA) **F:** State Street compensation: $325,005 (2021), State Street share value: $1 million (2021); HSBC shares sold in 2014 for $22.6 million

JULIO A. PORTALATIN, US
CB: State Street, SERVPRO **PE:** Marsh & McLennan Companies, Mercer Consulting Group, Chartis growth economies, AIG Europe, American International Underwriters, DXC Technology **PC:** World Economic Forum, AARP, Covenant House International, Hofstra University **E:** Hofstra University (BS) **F:** State Street compensation: $352,552 (2021), State Street share value: $215,950 (2021)

JOHN B. RHEA, US
CB: State Street; Invitation Homes; partner, Centerview Partners; founder and managing partner, RHEAL Capital Management **PE:** CEO, New York City Housing Authority; corporate finance and capital markets, Siebert Williams Shank & Co.; Boston Consulting Group; Lehman Brothers **PC:** Wesleyan University, American Red Cross Greater New York, University of Detroit Jesuit School **E:** Harvard Business School (MBA), Wesleyan University (BA) **F:** State Street compensation: $360,486 (2021), State Street share value: $315,691 (2021); Centerview Partners compensation: $424,066

RICHARD P. SERGEL, US

CB: State Street, Emera **PE:** President and CEO, New England Electric System (National Grid USA); North American Electric Reliability Corporation **PC:** Consortium for Energy Efficiency, Clean Air Task Force, Greater Boston Chamber of Commerce **E:** University of Miami (MBA), North Carolina State University (MS in applied mathematics), Florida State University (BS) **F:** State Street compensation: $319,823 (2021), State Street share value: $5.2 million (2021); Emera compensation: $320,402 (2021), Emera share value: $2.3 million (2021)

GREGORY L. SUMME, US

CB: State Street, Avantor, NXP Semiconductors, Virgin Orbit Holdings **PE:** AlliedSignal (Honeywell International); General Aviation Avionics; General Aviation; global buyout, Carlyle Group; Goldman Sachs Capital Partners; PerkinElmer; General Electric; LMI Aerospace; McKinsey **PC:** Conference Board **E:** Wharton School of the University of Pennsylvania (MBA), University of Cincinnati (MS), University of Kentucky (BS) **F:** State Street compensation: $325,552 (2021), State Street share value: $7.4 million (2021); Avantor compensation: $292,503 (2022), Avantor share value: $306,732 (2022); NXP Semiconductors compensation: $335,289 (2022), NXP Semiconductors share value: $2.2 million (2022); Virgin Orbit Holdings share value: $13 million (2022)

UBS
Twelve directors, AUM $4.38 trillion
REVENUE: $34.6 billion (2022)

Titan Cross-Investors in 2022:
BlackRock	$98.6 million
Vanguard	$45 million
State Street	$25 million

COLM KELLEHER, Ireland

CB: Chair: UBS; director, Norfolk Southern **PE:** Morgan Stanley **PC:** Director, Bretton Woods Committee; World Economic Forum; Swiss Finance Council; Americans for Oxford; Oxford Chancellor's Court of Benefactors; British Museum; International China Securities Regulatory Commission; European Financial Services Round Table; European Banking Group; International Monetary Conference **E:** Oxford University (MA) **F:** Norfolk Southern compensation: $305,120 (2022), Norfolk Southern share value: $644,176 (2022); UBS compensation: $5.3 million (2022)

LUKAS GÄHWILER, Switzerland

CB: UBS, Pilatus Aircraft, Ringier **PE:** Chair and president, UBS Switzerland; member of the Group Executive Board of UBS Group; chief credit officer, Global Private and Corporate Banking, Credit Suisse **PC:** Zürich Opera House; vice chairman, Swiss Bankers Association; chair, Employers Association of Banks in Switzerland; Economiesuisse; chair of the board, UBS Pension Fund; member, UBS Foundation of Economics in Society; member of the board, Swiss Finance Council **E:** Harvard Business School (Advanced Management Program), International Bankers School (MBA), Eastern Switzerland University of Applied Sciences, St. Gallen (BA) **F:** UBS compensation: $2.1 million (2022)

JEREMY ANDERSON, UK

CB: Chair, UBS; director, Prudential **PE:** Chair, global financial services, KPMG International; member of the Group Management Board and head of UK operations, Atos Origin **PC:** Trustee, UK's Productivity Leadership Group; World Economic Forum; trustee, Kingham Hill Trust; trustee, St. Helen's Bishopsgate **E:** University College London (BA) **F:** UBS compensation: $850,000 (2021–2022), UBS share value: $395,677 (2021–2022); Prudential compensation: $306,000 (2021)

CLAUDIA BÖCKSTIEGEL, Switzerland & Germany
CB: UBS; enlarged executive committee, Roche **PE:** Head of legal diagnostics, Roche in Basel, Switzerland; Roche Group **PC:** World Economic Forum **E:** Universities of Mannheim (JD) and Heidelberg (MA), Georgetown University (LL.M) **F:** UBS compensation: $300,000 (2021–2022), UBS share value: $139,636

WILLIAM C. DUDLEY, US
CB: UBS, Bank for International Settlements, Treliant **PE:** President and CEO, Federal Reserve Bank of New York (2009–2018); Goldman Sachs; executive VP, Morgan Guaranty Trust Company **PC:** Federal Open Market Committee; Council on Foreign Relations; World Economic Forum; Group of Thirty; Partnership for New York City; Trilateral Commission; chair, Bretton Woods Committee; committee chair, Economic Club of New York; economist, Federal Reserve Board; senior adviser, Griswold Center for Economic Policy Studies at Princeton University; board member, Council for Economic Education **E:** University of California, Berkeley (PhD), New College of Florida (BA) **F:** UBS compensation: $650,000 (2021–2022), UBS share value: $302,664 (2021–2022); Federal Reserve compensation: at least $400,000 (2016); net worth: $8.5 million (*New York Times*, November 5, 2017)

PATRICK FIRMENICH, Switzerland
CB: UBS; Jacobs Holding; chair, Firmenich International **PE:** CEO and vice chairman, Firmenich International **PC:** Board member, INSEAD and INSEAD World Foundation; World Economic Forum; advisory council member, Swiss Board Institute **E:** University of Geneva (MA), INSEAD Fontainebleau (MBA) **F:** UBS compensation: $550,000 (2021–2022), UBS share value: $487,404; Firmenich family net worth: $3.8 billion (2022)

FRED HU, China

CB: UBS; Ant Group; ICBC; Minsheng Financial Leasing; founder, chair, and CEO, Primavera Capital Group; chair, Yum China Holdings; codirector, National Center for Economic Research **PE:** Partner and chair for Greater China, Goldman Sachs; adjunct professor, Tsinghua University **PC:** Trustee, China Medical Board; governor, Chinese International School in Hong Kong; World Economic Forum; global adviser, Council on Foreign Relations; co-chairman, the Nature Conservancy's Asia Pacific Council; member of Board of Trustees of the Institute for Advanced Study; director and member of executive committee, China Venture Capital and Private Equity Association **E:** Harvard University (PhD, MA), Tsinghua University (MS) **F:** UBS compensation: $600,000 (2021–22), UBS share value: $412,117 (2021–22); net worth: $979 million[1]

MARK HUGHES, Canada & UK

CB: UBS; senior adviser, McKinsey **PE:** Chief risk officer and member of the Group Executive Committee, Royal Bank of Canada (retired 2018); visiting lecturer, University of Leeds **PC:** Chair, Global Risk Institute; World Economic Forum **E:** University of Manchester (MBA), University of Leeds (LLB) **F:** UBS compensation: $700,000 (2021–2022), UBS share value: $325,841 (2021–2022); Global Risk Institute compensation: $175,000 (2022)

NATHALIE RACHOU, France

CB: UBS, Euronext, Veolia Environnement, Société Générale **PE:** Senior adviser, Clartan Associés; founding partner and CEO, Topiary Finance **PC:** African Financial Institutions Investment Platform, World Economic Forum **E:** HEC Paris (MA), INSEAD Fontaineb-

---

leau (MBA) **F:** UBS compensation: $500,000 (2021–2022), UBS share value: $232,738 (2021–2022)[1]

JULIE G. RICHARDSON, US

CB: UBS, Datadog, Fivetran, Yext, Kroll Risk & Compliance Solutions (private), US Investigations Services **PE:** Arconic, Providence Equity Partners, Hartford Financial Services Group, JPMorgan Chase, Merrill Lynch, Open Solutions, SunGard, Stream Global Services **PC:** Make-A-Wish Foundation New York **E:** University of Wisconsin–Madison (BBA), Stanford Graduate School of Business **F:** UBS compensation: $800,000 (2021–2022), UBS share value: $372,392 (2021–2022); Datadog compensation: $257,279 (2022), Datadog share value: $4.8 million (2022); Yext compensation: $210,487 (2022), Yext shares: 225,532, value: $1.4 million (2022)

DIETER WEMMER, Switzerland & Germany

CB: UBS **PE:** CFO, Allianz; Zurich Insurance Group **PC:** CFO Forum; European Central Bank; Systemic Risk Working Group, Bank for International Settlements; Berlin Center of Corporate Governance; World Economic Forum; Economic and Finance Committee, Insurance Europe **E:** University of Cologne (PhD in mathematics, MA) **F:** UBS compensation: $700,000 (2021–2022), UBS share value: $325,841 (2021–2022); Allianz compensation: approximately $240,000 (2021)

JEANETTE WONG, Singapore

CB: UBS; Prudential; Singapore Airlines; Risk Committee, GIC; Jurong Town Corporation; PSA International **PE:** Group executive and CFO, DBS Bank **PC:** Chair, CareShield Life Council; Securities Industry Council; World Economic Forum **E:** University of Chicago

---

(MBA), National University of Singapore (BA) **F:** UBS compensation: $325,841 (2021–2022), UBS share value: $446,535 (2021–2022); Prudential compensation: $123,000 (2022); Singapore Airlines compensation: $99,000 (2021)

JPMORGAN CHASE
Eleven directors, AUM $2.9 trillion
REVENUE: $132.3 billion (2022)

Titan Cross-Investors in 2022:

Vanguard	$70.3 billion
BlackRock	$18.7 billion
State Street	$18.5 billion
Capital Group	$14.4 billion
Fidelity Investments	$9.5 billion
Morgan Stanley	$4.8 billion

LINDA B. BAMMANN, US
CB: JPMorgan Chase **PE:** Manulife Finance (Delaware), Bank One, UBS Warburg, Manulife Financial Corporation **PC:** Freddie Mac, Risk Management Association **E:** University of Michigan (MA), Stanford University (BS) **F:** JPMorgan compensation: $405,000 (2022), JPMorgan shares: 94,322, value: $12.4 million (2022)

STEPHEN B. BURKE, US
CB: JPMorgan Chase, Berkshire Hathaway **PE:** American Broadcasting Company; senior EVP, Comcast Corporation; CEO, NBCUniversal; Walt Disney Company **PC:** Emeritus trustee, Children's Hospital of Philadelphia **E:** Harvard Business School (MBA), Colgate University (BA) **F:** JPMorgan compensation: $452,500 (2022), JPMorgan shares: 237,113, value: $31 million (2022), Berkshire Hathaway compensation: $2,100 (2022); Berkshire Hathaway shares:

28, value: $12.8 million (2022)

TODD A. COMBS, US

CB: JPMorgan Chase, Charter Brokerage, Duracell, Berkshire Hathaway, Precision Castparts Corp. **PE:** Castle Point Capital Management, Chase Bank USA, Progressive Insurance, Copper Arch Capital **PC:** Florida Office of Financial Regulation **E:** Columbia Business School (MBA), Florida State University (BS) **F:** JPMorgan compensation: $394,755 (2022), JPMorgan share value: $3.5 million (2022); Berkshire Hathaway compensation: $1 million-plus, $27 million bonus (2013)[1]

JAMES S. CROWN (died, June 25, 2023, in a race car accident), US

CB: JPMorgan Chase, Henry Crown and Company, General Dynamics, Hillshire Brands (Sara Lee) **PE:** Salomon Brothers, Capital Markets Service Group, Hillshire Brands **PC:** World Business Chicago; PEC Israel Economic Corporation; trustee, the Aspen Institute; University of Chicago; trustee, Jewish Federation/Jewish United Fund of Metropolitan Chicago; trustee, Museum of Science and Industry Chicago; trustee, University of Chicago Medical Center **E:** Stanford University Law School (JD), Hampshire College (BA) **F:** JPMorgan compensation: $395,000 (2022), JPMorgan shares: 12,486,768, value: $1.6 billion (2022) (includes shares owned by Mr. Crown and his wife and children); General Dynamics compensation: $358,329 (2021), General Dynamics shares: 15.5 million, value: $330 million (2021); Hillshire compensation: $449,296 (2012), Hillshire shares: 23,705, value: $8.2 million; heir to $4 billion-plus Crown family fortune

1. Anupreeta Das, "Buffett Aides Score Big Payday," *Wall Street Journal*, May 2, 2013.

JAMES (JAMIE) DIMON, US

CB: JPMorgan Chase **PE:** Citigroup, Travelers Group, Commercial Credit Company, American Express, Salomon Smith Barney International, UnitedHeath Group **PC:** The Federal Reserve Bank of New York; World Economic Forum (2020); Business Roundtable; the Business Council; Council on Foreign Relations; Wall Street Journal CEO Council; trustee, New York University Medical Center; trustee, Harvard Business School **E:** Harvard Business School (MBA), Tufts University (BA) **F:** JPMorgan compensation: $84.4 million (2022), JPMorgan shares: 12,790,959, value: $1.2 billion (2022); net worth: $1.6 billion (*Forbes*)

TIMOTHY P. FLYNN, US

CB: JPMorgan Chase, UnitedHealth Group **PE:** Alcoa; Chubb; chairman, KPMG; Walmart **PC:** International Business Council, World Economic Forum; Business Roundtable; Financial Accounting Standards Board; the Prince of Wales's International Integrated Reporting Committee **E:** University of St. Thomas (BA) **F:** JPMorgan compensation: $515,000 (2022), JPMorgan shares: 61,068, value: $8 million (2022); Walmart compensation: $300,550 (2022), Walmart shares: 42,462, value: $6.1 million (2022); UnitedHealth Group compensation: $374,350 (2021), UnitedHealth Group share value: $5.3 million (2021)

ALEX GORSKY, US

CB: JPMorgan Chase, Apple, IBM, Johnson & Johnson **PE:** Chairman and CEO, Johnson & Johnson **PC:** Business Council; World Economic Forum; advisory council, New York Stock Exchange Board; New York-Presbyterian Hospital; Travis Manion Foundation; Board of Advisors, Wharton School of the University of Pennsylvania **E:** United States Military Academy West Point (BS), Wharton School of the University of Pennsylvania (MBA) **F:** Apple shares:

486, value: $64,297; IBM compensation: $564,084 (2021), IBM share value: $3,295,387 (2021); Johnson & Johnson compensation: $26.74 million (2021), Johnson & Johnson share value: $12.4 million (2021); JPMorgan compensation: $51,875 (2022)

MELLODY HOBSON, US
CB: JPMorgan Chase; president, Ariel Investments; Starbucks; the Rise Fund (AUM $7.2 billion) **PE:** Director, the Estée Lauder Companies; director, DreamWorks Animation **PC:** Director, Chicago Public Education Fund; chair, After School Matters; World Economic Forum; Executive Committee, Investment Company Institute's Board of Governors; board member of the George Lucas Education Foundation; vice chair of World Business Chicago; trustee, the Field Museum; board, Rockefeller Foundation; the Economic Club of Chicago **E:** Princeton University (BA) **F:** JPMorgan compensation: $397,500 (2022), JPMorgan share value: $1.9 million; Starbucks compensation: $479,949, Starbucks share value: $86 million

MICHAEL A. NEAL, US
CB: JPMorgan Chase, GE Capital, Acasta Enterprises **PE:** Vice chair, General Electric; CEO, GE Capital **PC:** US Advisory Board, the European Institute of Business Administration (INSEAD); World Economic Forum; Financial Services Forum; Georgia Tech Foundation **E:** Georgia Institute of Technology (BS) **F:** JPMorgan compensation: $380,000 (2022), JPMorgan shares: 48,962, value: $6.4 million (2022)

PHEBE N. NOVAKOVIC, US
CB: JPMorgan Chase, General Dynamics **PE:** President and CEO, General Dynamics (formerly EVP for marine systems, SVP of planning and development, and VP for strategic planning); director, Abbott Laboratories; assistant to the deputy secretary of

defense, Office of Management and Budget; operations officer, CIA **PC:** World Economic Forum; Project HOPE; trustee, Northwestern University; John F. Kennedy Center for the Performing Arts **E:** Wharton School of the University of Pennsylvania (MBA), Smith College (BA) **F:** JPMorgan compensation: $380,000 (2021), JPMorgan share value: $518,839 (2021); General Dynamics compensation: $23.5 million (2021), General Dynamics share value: $170 million

VIRGINIA M. ROMETTY, US

CB: JPMorgan Chase **PE:** CEO, IBM (retired 2020); AIG **PC:** Brookings Institution; Business Roundtable; Council on Foreign Relations; World Economic Forum; Peterson Institute for International Economics; trustee, Northwestern University (BS); Board of Overseers and Managers, Memorial Sloan Kettering Cancer Center; Alfalfa Club **E:** Northwestern University **F:** JPMorgan compensation: $380,000, JPMorgan share value: $690,540; IBM compensation: $20.1 million (2019), IBM shares: 437,531, value $39.5 million (2020)

ALLIANZ GROUP
Eleven directors, AUM $4.8 trillion (includes PIMCO)
REVENUE: $129.28 billion (2022)

Titan Cross-Investors in 2022:

Vanguard	$259.6 million
Amundi	$139 million
BlackRock	$130.3 million

OLIVER BÄTE, Germany

CB: CEO, Allianz **PE:** Westdeutsche Landesbank; McKinsey; German Air Force; professor, University of Cologne **PC:** Chairman,

European Insurance CFO Forum; World Economic Forum (2020); global adviser, Council on Foreign Relations; Council for Inclusive Capitalism (Vatican) **E:** New York University (MBA), University of Cologne **F:** Allianz compensation: $9.2 million (2022), Allianz shares: 14,154, value: $30.5 million (2022)

SERGIO BALBINOT, Italy
CB: Allianz, UniCredit, La Centrale Finanziaria Generale, Bajaj Allianz, Participatie Maatschappij Graafschap Holland, Generali Switzerland, Deutsche Vermögensberatung **PE:** Generali Insurance, Norddeutscher Lloyd **PC:** President, CEA (European insurance and reinsurance federation); Europ Assistance; European Financial Services Round Table; World Economic Forum **E:** University of Bologna (MBA, BA) **F:** Allianz compensation: $4.5 million (2021), Allianz shares: 6,710, value $1.4 million (2022); UniCredit compensation: $96,400; purchased $50.9 million in Allianz shares (2020)

SIRMA BOSHNAKOVA, Bulgaria
CB: Allianz **PE:** CEO, Uralsib Non-Life Insurance (P&C); Renaissance Insurance Group; Remedium Group; the Boston Consulting Group **PC:** World Economic Forum **E:** Moscow State Institute of International Affairs (PhD, MA) **F:** Allianz compensation: $4.2 million (2022), Allianz shares: 2,277, value: $491,832 (2022)

BARBARA KARUTH-ZELLE, Germany
CB: Allianz **PE:** Institute of Health Economics, Curatorship for Dialysis and Kidney Transplantation, Allianz Technology **PC:** Business Innovation Summit (London, 2022), World Economic Forum, Euler Hermes **E:** Universität der Bundeswehr (PhD), Ludwig-Maximilians-Universität (PhD in economics and business administration) **F:**

Allianz compensation: $4.4 million (2022), Allianz shares: 3,305, value: $713,880 (2022)

KLAUS-PETER RÖHLER, Germany
CB: Allianz, Eurokai **PE** Allianz Italy (1996) **E:** Göttingen University (PhD in law, MA in business administration), Vereins-und Westbank Hannover (bank apprenticeship) **F:** Allianz compensation: $4.4 million (2022), Allianz shares: 5,396, value: $1.1 million (2022)

IVAN DE LA SOTA, Spain
CB: Allianz, Volkswagen Autoversicherung **E:** University of Augsburg (MBA), City University Business School (MBA) **F:** Allianz compensation: $3.9 million (2022), Allianz shares: 6,077, value: $1.3 million (2022); Volkswagen Autoversicherung compensation: $363,733 (2022)

GIULIO TERZARIOL, Italy
CB: Allianz **PE:** Allianz Life Insurance Company of North America, Allianz Insurance Management Asia Pacific, Generali Insurance **E:** Luigi Bocconi University (MA), University of Cologne (Scholarships PIM/CEMS) **F:** Allianz compensation: $4.5 million (2022), Allianz shares: 6,537, value: $1.4 million (2022)

GÜNTHER THALLINGER, Austria
CB: Allianz **PE:** Technical University of Vienna, McKinsey **PC:** European Business Council, World Economic Forum (2020), Federal Finance Ministry, Principles for Responsible Investment Association, German Equity Institute, UN Net-Zero Emissions Commitments of Non-State Entities, UN-convened Net-Zero Asset Owner Alliance **E:** Technical University of Vienna (PhD, dissertation in applied mathematics), Technical University of Graz and Technical Univer-

sity of Vienna (MSc) **F:** Allianz compensation: $4.5 million (2022), Allianz shares: 6,562, value: $1.4 million (2022)[1]

CHRISTOPHER TOWNSEND, UK
CB: Allianz **PE:** AIG, AIG Asia Pacific, American Home Assurance Company, AIG South East Asia & Greater China Regional Holding Company, MetLife **PC:** Board, the Japan Society; adviser, the Asia Society; vice chairman, U.S.-Korea Business Council; international advisory council to the Guangdong government **E:** Chartered Insurance Institute, UK **F:** Allianz compensation: $4.5 million (2022), Allianz shares: 2,040, value: $440,640 (2022)

RENATE WAGNER, Romania & Germany
CB: Allianz, UniCredit **PE:** Westdeutsche Landesbank, KPMG AG Wirtschaftsprüfungsgesellleschaft, DAB Bank, Zurich Insurance Group, Allianz at Munich, Singapore, and Deutschland **PC:** Institute for Banking Innovation, World Economic Forum (2020) **E:** Heriot-Watt University (MBA), University of Paderborn (MA, mathematics) **F:** Allianz compensation: $4.5 million (2022), Allianz shares: 4,266, value: $899,856 (2022); UniCredit compensation: $150,000 (2022)

ANDREAS WIMMER, Germany
CB: Allianz, Pensions-Sicherungs-Verein, Allianz Lebensversicherungs **PE:** Researcher, the Institute for Banking Innovation; various positions, Allianz Lebensversicherungs, Versicherungs,

---

1. Günther Thallinger is also chair of the UN-convened Net-Zero Asset Owner Alliance (AOA), an organization of seventy-one asset owners, including some of the world's largest pension and sovereign wealth funds, with more than $10 trillion in assets under management. "The AOA members are not only committed to transitioning their portfolios to net-zero greenhouse gas (GHG) emissions by 2050. 29 of the 71 members have already set interim targets for 2025. More members are working on short term targets," Thallinger said, according to Allianz. "Such short term and interim targets are necessary to enforce the integration of climate impact in decision making. With such enhanced decision making, asset owners can help drive the necessary transformation of the economy." See "Günther Thallinger Joins New United Nations Advisory Council Focused on Accelerating Climate Action," Allianz SE, April 1, 2022.

and Deutschland **PC:** World Economic Forum **E:** University of Regensburg (PhD, BA), Murray State University (MBA) **F:** Allianz compensation: $4.3 million (2022), Allianz shares: 2,150, value: $464,400 (2022)

AMUNDI
Fifteen directors, AUM $5.01 trillion
(includes Crédit Agricole)
REVENUE: $3.4 billion (2022)

Titan Cross-Investors in 2022:

Crédit Agricole	$8.98 trillion
BlackRock	$129 million
Vanguard	$98.8 million
Fidelity Investments	$45.2 million

VALÉRIE BAUDSON, France
CB: CEO, Amundi; Executive Committee, Crédit Agricole Cheuvreux **PE:** Deputy CEO, Crédit Agricole; various positions, Amundi; chair of the supervisory board, Anatec; Banque Indosuez; Indosuez Wealth Management (2019) **PC:** French Financial Management Association, president of Paris Europlace Investors' College, World Economic Forum, CPR Asset Management **E:** HEC Paris (specialty in finance), Company Directorship Certificate from the Sciences Po-IFA University in Paris **F:** Amundi compensation: $974,820 (2022), Amundi shares: 5,169, value: $336,812 (2023); Crédit Agricole Cheuvreux shares: 1,930,615, value: $208 million

YVES PERRIER, France
CB: Chair, Edmond de Rothschild (since 2023) **PE:** Chair, Amundi; CEO, Amundi (2010–2021); chair and CEO, Crédit Agricole Asset Management (2007); CFO, Société Générale (1987); CFO, Crédit

Lyonnais (1999); World Economic Forum (2020); director, Euro Securities Partners **PC:** Vice chair of the board, Paris Europlace; chair, Comité Médicis, for socially responsible investment in France (2019); director, LCH.Clearnet and LCH.Clearnet Group (2015–20); French Legion of Honour, French National Order of Merit **E:** École Supérieure des Sciences Economiques et Commerciales (chartered accountant) **F:** Amundi salary: $398,936 (2022)

PHILIPPE BRASSAC, France

CB: Honorary chair of the board, Amundi; CEO, Crédit Agricole (since May 2015); Executive Committee, Crédit Agricole **PE:** Crédit Agricole (since 1982); World Economic Forum (2016–17); Cassa di Risparmio di Parma e Piacenza **PC:** Chair, French Banking Association; European Financial Services Round Table's Chevalier de la Légion d'Honneur **E:** École Nationale de la Statistique et de l'Administration Économique (MA in mathematics) **F:** Amundi compensation: $2.5 million (2023), Amundi shares: 200, value: $13,054

VIRGINIE CAYATTE, France

CB: Amundi; PagesJaunes; financial director, Adisseo; CFO, Adisseo (2015–present) **PE:** French Treasury (2002–7); director of finance, AXA IM (2010–15); CFO, Solocal **E:** École Nationale Supérieure des Mines de Paris (MS), École Polytechnique (Certificat d'administrateur de société, MA in economics/mathematics) **F:** Amundi compensation: $1.2 million, director compensation: $43,132; AXA compensation: $2 million (2018)

LAURENCE DANON ARNAUD, France

CB: Amundi, Groupe Bruxelles Lambert, Gecina **PE:** Director of corporate finance, Edmond de Rothschild; chair and CEO, Printemps; CEO, Bostik; chair, Leonardo & Co; director, Diageo (2006–15); Plastic

Omnium (2003–10); Experian (2007–10); Rhodia (2008–11); supervisory board, BPCE (2009–13); Total Fina Elf **PC:** President, École Normale Supérieure (Paris) Foundation; officer, French Legion of Honour **E:** École Normale Supérieure de Paris (physical science degree), École Nationale Supérieure des Mines (MS, engineering) **F:** Amundi compensation: $47,000; Gecina compensation: $66,278 (2022) (estimate based on ten directors sharing $773,255); Groupe Bruxelles Lambert compensation: $80,600 (2022); net worth: $5 million (2023)[1]

CHRISTINE GANDON, France
CB: Amundi; Camca; Crédit Agricole Italia; Crédit Agricole Leasing & Factoring; supervisory board, Crédit Agricole Titres **PE:** Sucreries du Nord; director, Caisse Locale de Fère-Champenoise and Sommesous **PC:** Chair of the Federal Treasury, ADMR **E:** Institut National Agronomique Paris-Grignon **F:** Amundi compensation: $441,906, Amundi shares: 200, value: $13,054

PATRICE GENTIÉ, France
CB: Amundi; chair, Caisse Régionale d'Aquitaine; Grand Sud-Ouest Capital; Foncaris **PE:** Crédit Agricole Group (1998); director, Caisse Locale de Sainte Livrade; director, Caisse Régionale du Lot-et-Garonne (1999–2001); Caisse Régionale d'Aquitaine; oenologist, Plaimont Group (1985) **PC:** Secretary general, French Federation of Vine Nurseries; director, Cerfrance 47 **E:** Bordeaux Sciences Agro (ENITA) (agricultural engineering and oenology) **F:** Amundi compensation: $15,489

MICHÈLE GUIBERT, France
CB: Amundi; CEO, Caisse Régionale des Côtes d'Armor; UNEXO; Indosuez Wealth Management **PE:** Crédit Agricole (2017); deputy CEO, Caisse Régionale de Crédit Agricole Toulouse (2012); Caisse

---

1. "Laurence Danon," Businessperson, Famous Birthdays, accessed August 28, 2023.

Régionale de Crédit Agricole Atlantique Vendée (2005) **PC:** Chair, the Village by CA, Côtes d'Armor; member of the Supervisory Board, Square Habitat Bretagne; member of the Transformation and Performance Committee and the Agriculture and Agri-Food Committee at FNCA **E:** Institut Technique de Banque (MA, applied mathematics and IT) **F:** Côtes d'Armor compensation: $636,517 (average); UNEXO compensation: $34,264; Indosuez compensation: $106,000; Amundi compensation: $37,618, Amundi shares: 200, value: $13,054

WILLIAM KADOUCH-CHASSAING, France
CB: Amundi; CFO, Eurazeo Group **PE:** JPMorgan (1998); Société Générale Corporate & Investment Banking; deputy CEO, Société Générale Group **PC:** Director, Université Sorbonne Nouvelle; Institut d'Etudes Politiques in Paris; chairman of the Ethics Committee, MEDEF (Movement of the Enterprises of France) (2008–13); chairman, Movement of Christian Entrepreneurs and Managers (Mouvement des Entrepreneurs et Dirigeants Chrétiens) (2010–14); vice chair of Fondation Notre Dame; honorary chair, Chambre Syndicale des Courtiers d'Assurance; chair of Fondation Avenir du Patrimoine à Paris **E:** École Normale Supérieure de Lyon (history, economics, sociology) **F:** Amundi compensation: $23,234, Amundi shares: 200, value: $13,054; Eurazeo Group compensation: $175,000 (average)

ROBERT LEBLANC, France
CB: Amundi; CEO, Aon France; International Space Brokers France; Aspen Institute France **PE:** CEO, Siaci; Apax France; AXA; Paris Stock Exchange; CEO, La Société des Bourses Françaises; CEO, Meeschaert Rousselle **PC:** Fondation Notre Dame; chair, Chambre Syndicale des Courtiers d'Assurance; Ethics Committee, MEDEF; French Center for Christian Employers; chair, Fondation Avenir du Patrimoine à Paris **E:** Université Paris Dauphine (PhD in organizational strategy), École

Polytechnique **F:** Amundi compensation: $49,234, Amundi shares: 200, value: $13,054; Aspen France compensation: $164,022 (average); Aon France compensation: $1.5 million

MICHEL MATHIEU, France
CB: Amundi; CEO, LCL Crédit Agricole; chair, Crédit Agricole Creditor; board, Eurazeo Insurance **PE:** Director, Predica; deputy CEO, Crédit Agricole (2010); director, CA Italia; CEO, Caisse Régionale du Midi (1995); Crédit Agricole Gard (1983); director, Crédit Agricole Egypt **PC:** President, Manège de Chaillot endowment fund **E:** University of Montpellier (PhD in corporate and business law) **F:** Amundi compensation: $23,234, Amundi shares: 200, value: $13,054; Eurazeo Insurance compensation: $175,000 (average)

ESTELLE MENARD, France
CB: Director, LCL Crédit Agricole **PE:** Employee director, Amundi; European equity manager and international equity manager, Amundi **PC:** deputy head of thematic equity management, CPR Asset Management **E:** DESS MA in Banking, Finance and International Trade, BA European Financial Analysis, Certificate in Company Directorship, Institut d'Etudes Politiques in Paris **F:** Amundi compensation: $19.9 million, Amundi share value: $45,218

HÉLÈNE MOLINARI, France
CB: Amundi; manager, Ahm Conseil; Be-Bound Inc.; Albingia (insurance); Lagardère Group **PE:** Supervisory Board, IDI (investments); AXA Asset Managers; Robeco Group; Capgemini **PC:** Chair, SUMus Venice (charity); chair, MEDEF (French employers federation) (2011); steering committee, Everyone Sings Against Cancer; director, Boyden Foundation **F:** Amundi compensation: $34,618, Amundi shares: 200, value: $13,054; Lagardère Group compensation: $14,546

XAVIER MUSCA, France

CB: Amundi (past chair 2016–21); CEO, Crédit Agricole; Predica; CA Assurances and CA Italia; Capgemini (2016); Capgemini SE (2014) **PE:** Secretary-General to the French president (2011); director, French Treasury (2004); cabinet of Prime Minister Édouard Balladur; French Treasury Directorate (1993); French Inspectorate-General for Finance (1985) **PC:** Chevalier in 2009, the Order of Merit, the Order of Agricultural Merit, Order of Charles III (Spain) **E:** Institut d'Etudes Politiques in Paris, École Nationale d'Administration **F:** Capgemini compensation: $82,000; Amundi compensation: $4,993, Amundi shares: 300, value: $19,575; Crédit Agricole compensation: $1.3 million, Crédit Agricole shares: 18,192, value: $107,878; net worth: $5 million[1]

CHRISTIAN ROUCHON, France

CB: Amundi; management committee, Caisse Regionale de Credit Agricole Mutuel de Sud Rhône-Alpes; CEO, Caisse Régionale de Crédit Agricole Group (2019); Crédit Agricole Corporate and Investment Bank (2020) **PE:** Chair, BforBank (2013–17); Supervisory Committee, Fonds CA Transitions (2010–17); Caisse Régionale Sud Rhône-Alpes (2006); Caisse Régionale Loire Haute-Loire, Crédit Agricole Group (1988) **E:** Institut d'Etrudes Politiques, Paris (CPA, Chartered Accountant, Accounting Expert Degree) **F:** Amundi compensation: $60,322, Amundi shares: 200, value: $13,054; CRCAM de Sud Rhône-Alpes compensation: $279,337; Caisse Régionale de Crédit Agricole Group compensation: $409,460

---

1. "Xavier Musca," Economist, Famous Birthdays, accessed August 28, 2023.

CAPITAL GROUP
Ten directors, AUM $2.7 trillion
REVENUE: $8 billion (2022)[1]

Note: Approximately 80 percent of privately held Capital
Group stock is owned by employees.[2]

Titan Cross-Investors in 2022:

Vanguard	$11.8 billion
BlackRock	$4.8 billion
State Street	$1.3 billion

BOARD OF DIRECTORS: 2022

Directors are mostly career executives at Capital with twenty to
thirty years of experience. All employees receive a 15 percent bonus in
retirement options and can buy Capital shares without fees.

TIMOTHY D. ARMOUR, US
CB: Capital Group **PE:** Various positions at Capital Group for
thirty-three years (starting 1983) **PC:** Pacific Region Board, Boys &
Girls Clubs of America; Board of Councilors, University of Southern
California Marshall School of Business **E:** Middlebury College (BA,
economics) **F:** Capital compensation: $265,000, Capital stock shares
worth an estimated $98 million[3]

CANISE ARREDONDO, US
CB: Capital Group (since 2008), Discovery Cube Los Angeles **PE:**
Various positions at Capital Group for twenty-five years, IndyMac

1. "Capital Group Companies," Profile, *Forbes*, accessed August 28, 2023].
2. Capital Group Companies, Inc. v. Armour, C.A. No. 422-N (Del. Ch. Oct. 29, 2004), 26.
3. Tom Petruno, "Case May Give View of Capital Group," *Los Angeles Times*, October 14, 2005.

Bank, Deloitte & Touche **E:** University of California, Santa Barbara (BA); Universidade Federal de Santa Catarina, Brazil (1989–1993) **F:** Capital average compensation: $212,000[1]

NORIKO CHEN, US

CB: Capital Group **PE:** Various positions at Capital Group for twenty-three years, Worldsec International Limited in Hong Kong, Mitsubishi Bank **PC:** Trustee, Williams College; Women's Foundation in Hong Kong; Bay Area Women's Sports Initiative in California **E:** Williams College (BA in economics), Keio University (Japanese Language Bekka Program) **F:** Capital average compensation: $212,000

MIKE GITLIN, US

CB: Capital Group (since 2015) **PE:** T. Rowe Price, Citigroup Global Markets, Credit Suisse Asset Management, George Weiss and Associates **PC:** Catch a Lift Fund **E:** Colgate University (BA) **F:** T. Rowe share value: $18.9 million; Capital average compensation: $212,000

JOANNA (JODY) JONSSON, US

CB: Capital Group (since 1990) **PE:** Various positions at Capital Group for thirty-three years, Fidelity Management & Research Company in Boston, Irving Trust Company in New York **PC:** CFA Institute, Stanford Graduate School of Business, American Enterprise Institute, Alpha USA, Angel Flight West **E:** Stanford Graduate School of Business (MBA), Princeton University (BA) **F:** Capital average compensation: $212,000

ROB KLAUSNER, US

CB: Capital Group (since 2011) **PE:** Various positions in Capital

---

1. "Capital Group Executive Salaries," Employee Salaries, Comparably, accessed August 28, 2023.

Group; Accenture **E:** Loyola Marymount University (BS) **F:** Capital average compensation: $212,000

ROBERT (ROB) W. LOVELACE, US

CB: Capital Group, New World Fund, New Perspective Fund **PE:** Various positions at Capital Group for thirty-three years (since 1985) **PC:** J. Paul Getty Trust, Pacific Council on International Policy, California Community Foundation, US Olympic & Paralympic Foundation, US Soccer Federation's Championship Circle **E:** Princeton University (BA) **F:** Capital average compensation: $212,000

GREG MILIOTES, US

CB: Capital Group, Management Committee, 17 years with Capital Group Equity portfolio, **PE:** Silverman Capital Management, RS Investments Management, **E:** Stanford University School of Business, MA & Certificate in Global Management, BA Mechanical Engineering, Massachusetts Institute of Technology, **F:** Capital average compensation: $212,000

MARTIN ROMO, US

CB: Chair, Capital Group (since 2023); the Growth Fund of America; the Investment Company of America **PC:** The Basic Fund, Jamestown Community Council **E:** Stanford Graduate School of Business (MBA), UC Berkeley (BA), **F:** Capital average compensation: $212,000

MATT O'CONNER, US

CB: Capital Group, Management Committee, 15 yeass with Capital Group, CEO of American Funds at Capital Group, **PE:** Putman Investments, **E:** Chartered Financial Analyst, MBA Babson College, BA, Saint Anselm College, **F:** Capital average compensation: $212,000

FIDELITY INVESTMENTS FMR
Three directors, AUM $4.5 trillion 2021
REVENUE: $25.2 billion (2022)

Johnson Family Owned 49% ($48 billion 2022)

ABIGAIL PIERREPONT JOHNSON, US
CB: President-CEO, Fidelity Financial Investment FMR **PE:** Booz Allen & Hamilton **PC:** Trustee of Fidelity Commonwealth Trust, Massachusetts Institute of Technology **E:** Harvard Business School (MBA), Hobart and William Smith Colleges (BA) **F:** Net worth $29.5 billion 2024

VICKI L. FULLER, US
CB: Board of Trustees, Fidelity Investment funds 2018-present, Treliant, Blackstone Credit Investments, Ariel Alternatives, Equity Alliance **PE:** CIO, New York State Common Retirement Fund; AllianceBernstein (27 years); Governance Committee of The Williams Companies; VP at Standard and Poor's; investment associate at Morgan Stanley **PC:** Roosevelt University Academic Affairs Council, Board NYU Stern School of Business, Board Robert Wood Johnson Foundation **E:** Harvard University (MBA), Roosevelt University (BA, BS), Certified Public Accountant **F:** Compensation Williams Companies, $270,000,

C. BRUCE JOHNSTONE, US
CB: Executive Vice President and Chairman of Investment Committee at Fidelity Investments FMR, AP Capital Partners **PC:** Needham Education Foundation, Harvard Business School Fund, Alexis de Tocqueville Society of the United Way, Inner City Schools Scholarship Fund, Named by Money Magazine in 1987 as Ameri-

ca's Best Income Investor, raised $180 million for Harvard Business School from 1998–2003 **E:** Harvard Business School (MBA), Harvard College (BA)

TITANS: THEIR CORPORATE BOARDS 2022
(n=133)

The Titans sit on the boards of directors of 133 independent corporations. These corporations have annual revenues ranging from $5 million to $324 billion, with an average revenue of $34.16 billion in 2022. The collective total annual revenue for these 133 corporations was greater than $4.54 trillion in 2022.

These companies are all directly linked by cross-board memberships, allowing for potential investment access to the $50 trillion managed by the top ten capital investment management companies. Networked to each other through board directorships of the 117 Titans, these 133 companies have a higher collective annual revenue than the gross domestic products for all nations in the world except the United States, China, and Japan.[1]

TITAN BOARD MEMBERSHIP COMPANIES IN 2022
(n=133)

Titans serve on the boards of some of the most powerful companies in the world, as indicated by the following list:

Abacai, Acasta Enterprises, Adisseo, Airbnb, Allied World Assurance Company, Albingia, America Telecom, AmerisourceBergen, Aon France, Ariel Investments, Apple,

---

1. "Top 15 Countries by GDP in 2022," Global PEO Services, accessed August 28, 2023.

Avantor, Aviva, Bank for International Settlements, Be-Bound, Bitsight, Bogle Small Cap Growth Fund, Banque Edmond de Rothschild, ByteDance, BlackIvy Group, Bell Canada, BP, Berkshire Hathaway, Carnival, CA Indosuez Wealth Management, Capgemini SE, CAP Gemini, CCS Holding, Centerview Partners, Cisco Systems, Charter Brokerage, Coca-Cola, CVS Health, Datadog, Discovery Cube Los Angeles, Dow Chemical, DTE Energy, DuPont de Nemours, Duracell, eBay, Edmond de Rothschild Holding, Elastic, Emera, EQT Corporation, the Estée Lauder Companies, Euronext, Eurokai, Eurazeo Group, GmbH, Fannie Mae, Freddie Mac, PNC Financial Services Group, Firmenich International, Fivetran, GE Capital, Gecina, GIC, Guardian Life Insurance Company of America, General Atlantic, General Dynamics, General Motors, Globality, Groupe Bruxelles Lambert, Grand Sud-Ouest Capital, Hamilton Insurance Group, Hillenbrand, Halliburton, Hillshire Brands, Henry Crown and Company, Hewlett-Packard, Hiscox, HighVista Strategies, IBM, iCruise.com, In-Q-Tel, Innovir Laboratories, Invitation Homes, Iron Mountain, KGaA, K2 Intelligence, Kinnevik, Kroll Risk & Compliance Solutions, Jacobs Holding, Johnson & Johnson, Jurong Town Corporation, Kyoto Fund, Lagardère Group, Land O'Lakes, Live Nation Entertainment, Macy's, Magic Leap, McKinsey, Merck, Mercedes-Benz Group, Mitsubishi UFJ Financial Group, Momentive Global, MUFG Bank, Norfolk Southern, NXP Semiconductors, PACCAR, Patheon, Pilatus Aircraft, Precision Castparts, Primavera Capital Group, PSA International, Prudential, Procter & Gamble, Publicis Groupe, RBB Fund, Ringier, RHEAL Capital Management, the Rise Fund, RIT Capital Partners, Roche Holding, Secureworks,

Sears Roebuck, SERVPRO, Sierra Space, Singapore Airlines, SKF, Shell, SL Advisory, Starbucks, Société Générale, SOSV, Treliant, UniCredit, US Commercial Corp., UnitedHealth Group, United States Steel, Unum Group, UNEXO, US Investigations Services, Verizon Communications, Valero Energy, Veolia Environnement, VEREIT, Yext, Volkswagen, Yum China Holdings, Wellington Management Group, Workiva, Xos, Zoetis, Zurich Insurance Group.

TITANS AS NATIONAL AND COMMUNITY POLICY ADVISERS

Titans take an active part in numerous local, national, and international policy groups, government councils, business-policy organizations, major nonprofit foundations, and university trusteeships. Many of the Titans also serve as advisers or trustees on a total of forty-six university boards and five educational nonprofits. Titans sit on ninety local, national, and international business-related policy and advisory boards and sixty-nine nonprofit boards and governmental advisory associations. They also serve on twenty-nine nonprofit arts and health boards and policy councils. Titans serve on a total of 234 boards and councils, mostly in the United States and Europe, with a few in Asia and other locations. Titans are widely involved in the mechanisms and policies of government, business, nonprofit organizations, and education in the United States, Europe, and around the world, with many double and triple overlaps of Titans serving the entities on the following list.

INTERNATIONAL POLICY GROUPS

Titans also serve as members of groups and organizations that establish international policy:

The Trilateral Commission, Bank for International Settlements, Atlantic Council (NATO), UN Foundation, International Monetary Fund, the Prince of Wales's International Integrated Reporting Committee, Global Advisory Council of Bank of America, Center for Strategic and International Studies, Asia-Pacific Economic Cooperation Business Advisory Council, Institute of International Finance, Pacific Council on International Policy, Royal Institute of International Affairs, British-American Business Council, China Securities Regulatory Commission, Systemic Risk Working Group, Million Dollar Round Table.

NATIONAL AND REGIONAL POLICY ORGANIZATIONS

Council on Foreign Relations, National Security Council, Federal Advisory Council (Federal Reserve Banks), European Business Leaders' Convention, the Business Council, Hedge Fund Standards Board, Financial Services Roundtable, Federal Reserve Bank of New York, Joint Economic Committee of Congress, the Conference Board, National Committee on US-China Relations, US Council for International Business, the Business Roundtable, United Nations Association of the USA, US Chamber of Commerce, Kuwait Fund for Arab Economic Development, Pennsylvania Business Council, National Association of Manufacturers, US Securities and

Exchange Commission, New York Board of the National Association of Corporate Directors, Financial Industry Regulatory Authority, Greater Boston Chamber of Commerce, Economic Club of New York, Committee on Capital Markets Regulation, American Institute of Certified Public Accountants, Financial Accounting Standards Board, New York Innovation Center, CEA (European insurance and reinsurance federation), European Insurance CFO Forum, European Banking Group, Swiss Bankers Association, Swiss Finance Council, Federal Reserve Board, Swiss Board Institute, China Venture Capital and Private Equity Association, Global Risk Institute, African Financial Institutions Investment Platform, CFO Forum, European Central Bank, Securities Industry Council, Freddie Mac, Fannie Mae, Risk Management Association, Florida Office of Financial Regulation, World Business Chicago, PEC Israel Economic Corporation, French Finance Association, Investment Company Institute's Board of Governors, Principles for Responsible Investment, German Equity Institute, UN High-Level Expert Group on the Net-Zero Emissions Commitments of Non-State Entities, American Enterprise Institute, G100 BoardExcellence, Wall Street Journal CEO Council, the Council for Inclusive Capitalism with the Vatican.

NONPROFITS AND NONGOVERNMENTAL ADVISERS

American Red Cross; Canadian Council of Chief Executives; Chicago Council on Global Affairs; Banking Counsel for the US Senate Committee on Banking, Housing, and Urban Affairs; Bretton Woods Committee; King Charles III Charitable Fund (formerly the Prince of Wales's Charitable Fund); State of Maryland; Memorial Sloan Kettering Cancer Center;

New York City; Partnership for New York City; UN Sustainable Development Solutions Network Leadership Council; UN Business and Sustainable Development Commission; United Way of Rochester; Rochester Urban League; Oxfam America; Lumina Foundation; Chief Executives for Corporate Purpose; Clinton Foundation; RoundTable Healthcare Partners; the Investment Fund for Foundations; James Madison Council of the Library of Congress; Kessler Foundation; International Accounting Standards Board; Public Company Accounting Oversight Board; Accounting Standards Oversight Council of Canada; SASB Foundation; Save the Children; All Stars Helping Kids; Balance Vector; the American Ditchley Foundation; the Ireland Funds; National Italian American Foundation; UK's Productivity Leadership Group; Kingham Hill Trust; St. Helen's Bishopsgate; INSEAD World Foundation; Make-A-Wish Foundation New York; Berlin Center of Corporate Governance; Insurance and Financial Services Committee; Tiger Woods Foundation; the Boston Foundation; Aspen Institute; Travis Manion Foundation; George Lucas Education Foundation; French Federation of Vine Nurseries; Cerfrance; Fondation Avenir du Patrimoine à Paris, French insurance broker association; Ethics Committee, MEDEF; French Confederation of Christian Workers; Manège de Chaillot endowment fund; Catch a Lift Fund; Alpha USA; J. Paul Getty Trust; California Community Foundation; Clean Air Task Force; Alfalfa Club.

UNIVERSITY TRUSTEES

Massachusetts Institute of Technology; New York University; London Business School; University of Chicago; Wharton

School of the University of Pennsylvania; Williams College; New York University Medical Center; Rockefeller University; Villanova University; Roosevelt University; Wesleyan University; Amherst College; Tsinghua University School of Economics and Management; Augustana College; University of Pennsylvania; Stanford Graduate School of Business; W. Edwards Deming Center for Quality, Productivity, and Competitiveness at Columbia Business School; University of Rochester; University of Southern California Marshall School of Business; University of Rochester Medical Center; Monroe Community College Foundation; North Carolina A&T State University's College of Engineering Industry Advisory Group; Colgate Rochester Crozer Divinity School; University of Notre Dame Kellogg Institute for International Studies; Council on Chicago Booth; Northwestern University; Dartmouth College; Graduate Management Admission Council; Williams College Center for Development Economics; Duke Kunshan University; Brandeis University; Windsor School; University of Texas at Austin McCombs School of Business; IYRS School of Technology & Trades; Syracuse University; Commissioner of the US–UK Fulbright Commission; Covenant House International; Hofstra University; University of Detroit Jesuit School; Princeton University Griswold Center for Economic Policy Studies; Council for Economic Education; Chinese International School in Hong Kong; Chicago Public Education Fund; After School Matters; Financial Services Forum; Georgia Tech Foundation; Peterson Institute for International Economics; Paris Europlace College of Institutional Investors; École Normale Supérieure (Paris) Foundation; Université Sorbonne Nouvelle, Institut d'Etudes Politiques in Paris; Fondation Notre Dame; NYU Stern Executive Education.

ARTS, HEALTH, AND ACTIVISM ORGANIZATIONS

Philadelphia Orchestra, World Wildlife Fund, Massachusetts General Hospital, Museum of Modern Art, Metropolitan Museum of Art, China Medical Board, WEF Partnership for Global LGBTI Equality (PGLE), Huntington's Disease Society of America, MS Society of Northern California, Whitaker Peace & Development Initiative, the Posse Foundation (university scholarships), NewYork-Presbyterian Hospital, the Carnegie Hall Corporation/The Andrew Carnegie Society, WBUR (public radio station in Boston), Nature Conservancy, AARP, Consortium for Energy Efficiency, CareShield Life Council, Square Habitat Bretagne, SUMus (Venice, Italy), Boys & Girls Clubs of America, Women's Foundation in Hong Kong, Bay Area Women's Sports Initiative in California, Angel Flight West, US Olympic & Paralympic Foundation, US Soccer Federation Championship Circle, Jamestown Community Council, Basic Fund

US POLITICAL DONATIONS BY TITANS

More than 80 percent of US-based Titans have donated to either one or both of the major political parties' candidates during the past twenty years. The exception to this is Capital Group, where only two board members were political donors. Those who are *not* citizens of the US—that is, European Titans—are *not* legally allowed to make political donations in the US.

Since the Supreme Court ruling on the *Citizens United v. Federal Election Commission* case, in 2010, which afforded wealthy individuals and corporations the unrestricted ability to make donations to political campaigns, billionaires can use their money for political activities that allow them to dominate the democratic process in the United States. A clear example of this is how multimillionaire Mellody Hobson, from JPMorgan Chase, donated $1.25 million to the Democratic Senate Majority PAC in the 2020 election cycle. Hobson also donated $360,000 to the Biden Action Fund in 2020 and $285,000 to the Democratic National Committee.[1]

TITAN PARTICIPATION ON ELITE US POLICY COUNCILS

The leading three business and international policy councils in the US are the Council on Foreign Relations, Business Roundtable, and the Business Council. These private groups heavily influence US federal government policies on the protection of concentrated global investment capital. These policy groups in turn have significant say in actions by the US government, military, and intelligence agencies—from foreign policy strategies to banking regulations—which work toward positive outcomes for the Titans of Capital and the $50 trillion of investment capital they control.

COUNCIL ON FOREIGN RELATIONS

Bankers and leading corporate officials in the United States founded the CFR in New York in 1921. Academics, diplomats, and lawyers interested in expanding US global interests quickly joined them. The CFR would form policy study groups and issue reports for widespread review. In 1939, with Rockefeller Foundation support, the council formed a series

---

1. "Senate Majority PAC," LittleSis (Public Accountability Initiative), accessed November 27, 2023.

of groups that led to the US postwar policy supporting an economic Grand Area plan for US hegemony that included Latin America, Europe, British colonies, Southeast Asia, and Japan. US interests aiming for economic domination promoted the formation of the United Nations, World Bank, and International Monetary Fund. Strong anticommunist beliefs among CFR members led to US military involvement in Vietnam.[1] The CFR continues to have a significant influence on US foreign policy, issuing reports on Iraq, Iran, Russia, and China over the past few decades. The council remains focused on US economic hegemony, with an emphasis on protecting US investment interests. CFR publishes *Foreign Affairs*, a policy journal released six times a year. Current membership: 5,220. Board of directors: 38. Global advisers: 25.

Titan members of CFR include:
Jami Miscik (Morgan Stanley), vice chair
James P. Gorman (Morgan Stanley), director
Larry Fink (BlackRock), past director
Oliver Bäte (Allianz), global adviser
Fred Hu (UBS), global adviser
Thomas H. Glocer (Morgan Stanley), featured member[2]
Jamie Dimon (JPMorgan Chase), featured member
Virginia M. Rometty (JPMorgan Chase), featured member
Shelley B. Leibowitz (Morgan Stanley), member
William C. Dudley (UBS), member
William E. Ford (BlackRock), member

---

1. Domhoff, *Who Rules America?*
2. A "featured member" is someone who has been granted a published interview on the CFR website.

BUSINESS ROUNDTABLE

Business Roundtable was founded in 1972 by anti-union corporate leaders. Several studies showed Business Roundtable to be at the center of the largest globalizing companies. The Roundtable website describes the group as "an association of more than 200 chief executive officers (CEOs) of America's leading companies, representing every sector of the US economy. Business Roundtable CEOs lead US-based companies that support one in four American jobs and almost a quarter of US GDP. Through CEO-led policy committees, Business Roundtable members develop and advocate directly for policies to promote a thriving US economy and expanded opportunity for all Americans." Business Roundtable was a driving force behind the creation of the North American Free Trade Agreement (NAFTA) and the designation of China as a nation of "permanent normal trade relations."[1]

Titan members of Business Roundtable:
Jamie Dimon (JPMorgan Chase), board of directors
Beth Ford (BlackRock), board of directors
Virginia M. Rometty, (JPMorgan Chase), board of directors
Larry Fink (BlackRock), member
Kristin Peck (BlackRock), member
James P. Gorman (Morgan Stanley), member
Dennis M. Nally (Morgan Stanley), corporate governance
Timothy P. Flynn, (JPMorgan Chase), corporate governance

---

1. Domhoff, *Who Rules America?*

THE BUSINESS COUNCIL

The Business Council was formed in 1933 as an advisory board to the White House on the labor crises of the Great Depression. Business leaders in the thirties feared the rise of radical labor-union movements. The Business Council took the lead on encouraging a corporate liberal approach to federal labor legislation, which led to the passage, in 1935, of the National Labor Relations Act and Social Security Act.[1]

The Business Council now comprises leaders of the largest US corporations. Participation is by invitation only, and there can be only two hundred members at a time. The Business Council offers policy advice to all levels of the federal government via policy reports and invitational banquets.[2]

Titan members of the Business Council:
Jamie Dimon (JPMorgan Chase)
William E. Ford (BlackRock)
James P. Gorman (Morgan Stanley)
Alex Gorsky (JPMorgan Chase)

TITANS IN US INTELLIGENCE

Two Titans, both women, have direct employment experience with the US Central Intelligence Agency. Phebe N. Novakovic, a director for JPMorgan Chase, worked for the CIA from 1997 to 2001, while married to Michael G. Vickers, who later served as under secretary of defense for intelligence and security during the Obama administration. In addition to being a

---

1. Peter Phillips, "The 1934–35 Red Threat," *Critical Sociology* 20 Number 2 (July 1994), 27–50.
2. Domhoff, *Who Rules America?*

CIA case officer, Novakovic served as assistant to the deputy secretary of defense, Office of Management and Budget. In 2001 she joined General Dynamics, and twelve years later she became its CEO. She has served as chair of the board since 2013. While working at General Dynamics, Novakovic met and married David Morrison, a top staffer in the House Appropriations Subcommittee on Defense. He went on to become a chief lobbyist for Boeing.[1]

General Dynamics is the fifth-largest defense contractor in the US and fifth in the world for arms sales. It produces Columbia-class nuclear submarines, Arleigh Burke–class guided-missile destroyers, M1 Abrams tanks, and Stryker armored vehicles. Worldwide sales in 2022 netted $39.4 billion.

Novakovic's earnings include JPMorgan Chase board compensation of $380,000 (for 2021), JPMorgan shares worth $518,839 (2021), General Dynamics compensation of $23.5 million (2021), and General Dynamics shareholdings worth $170 million.

The second CIA Titan is Judith (Jami) A. Miscik, who serves on Morgan Stanley's board. Miscik worked for the CIA from 1983 to 2005 and was its deputy director of intelligence from 2005 to 2008. In 2009, Miscik joined Kissinger Associates, an international consulting firm, as its CEO. She also served on the President's Intelligence Advisory Board from 2009 to 2017.

Miscik serves on the boards of directors of General Motors and In-Q-Tel. In-Q-Tel is a Virginia-based venture capital nonprofit firm that equips the CIA and other intelligence agencies with the most up-to-date intelligence technologies. She also serves on the National Security Council, chairs the American

---

1. Carla Anne Robbins, "The Spy in General Dynamics' Corner Office," *Fortune*, September 11, 2015.

Ditchley Foundation, serves with the United Nations Association, and is a director of the Council on Foreign Relations. Miscik held more than $2.5 million in Morgan Stanley stock in 2022, when her Morgan Stanley compensation was $370,000. Her GM compensation was $361,660 in 2020, and in 2022 she held more than 7,800 GM shares, valued at $283,536.

TITANS: A SOCIOECONOMIC PROFILE[1]

A typical Titan from among the 117 listed in this book is a married heterosexual man or woman with children, is fifty-five to seventy years of age, and holds assets valued between $5 million and $20 million. They were born in the United States or Europe, raised in a wealthy, professional family, and attended an elite private university. They hold a master's or law degree. They serve on the boards of directors of two or more publicly traded corporations, earning more than $400,000 for that service in addition to lucrative stock options. They serve two or more social policy groups or cultural organizations.

Serving as a director of one of the top ten investment companies is a position they obtained after a successful career as a CEO or high-level corporate official with access to and awareness of capital investment funds. They take seriously their fiduciary responsibility to maximize returns on the capital investments under their control. Those who vote in the United States are likely members of the Republican Party or Democrats who are strongly probusiness. They believe in a capitalist system of free enterprise and view socialism and communism as abhorrent global threats. They are generally aware of the socio-

---

1. This profile is a qualitative statement based on the author's hundreds of hours of research on the 117 Titans identified in this book.

environmental threats posed by climate change but believe that effective mitigations can be developed without limiting investment returns on global capital. They support a strong US military with justified obligations to NATO allies and believe that the World Economic Forum's stakeholder capitalism, discussed in the following chapter, is the solution to promoting global human rights and social betterment.

CHAPTER 3

THE WORLD ECONOMIC FORUM
Saviors of Capitalism—and Climate-Crisis Profiteers

Starting in 1971 with 450 participants, the annual World Economic Forum meetings in Davos, Switzerland, have hosted 2,500 to 3,000 top government officials and high-level personnel from the largest thousand corporations in the world, along with famous cultural figures and celebrities. Seventy-six Titans (65 percent) are actively engaged with the World Economic Forum. BlackRock CEO and billionaire Larry Fink serves as a WEF trustee.

In his book *Davos Man*, Peter S. Goodman, a global economics correspondent for the *New York Times*, describes how, at Davos, "the most powerful people gather together behind closed doors, without any accountability, and they write the rules for the rest of the world."[1]

The World Economic Forum describes itself as "the international organization for public-private cooperation." According to its website, the WEF "engages the foremost political, business and other leaders of society to shape global, regional and industry agendas" and it characterizes itself as "independent,

---

1. Peter S. Goodman, *Davos Man: How the Billionaires Devoured the World* (New York: HarperCollins Publishers, 2023), 6.

impartial and not tied to any special interests. . . . Moral and intellectual integrity is at the heart of everything it does."[1]

Attending the Davos sessions are CEOs and representatives from the top one thousand billion-dollar corporations in the world, numerous heads of state and finance ministers, and leaders of major policy organizations, nonprofits, and important financial and governmental institutions such as the World Bank, International Monetary Fund, European Central Bank, United Nations, and NATO.[2]

The WEF continually highlights the problems of global economic inequality; environmental degradation, including the climate crisis; and other major socioeconomic problems. The January 2017 meeting promoted Davos leaders' reflections on "social divides." One report from that year declared that elites must not isolate themselves from the rest of the world. Philip Jennings of UNI Global Union stated that "if we want to create a society that works for all, everyone must have a seat at the decision-making table, in some capacity."[3]

The founder of WEF, Klaus Schwab, has described his core philosophical beliefs for a better capitalism. Schwab calls for "stakeholder capitalism," whereby corporations take a moral position to protect not only their own profits but also the world's people from mass inequality and environmental devastation.[4]

In fall 2019, the US Business Roundtable officially endorsed stakeholder capitalism. Jamie Dimon, chair of the Business Council and CEO of JPMorgan Chase, stated, "The American Dream is alive, but fraying. Major employers are investing in

---

1. "Our Mission," About, World Economic Forum, accessed August 28, 2023.
2. World Economic Forum, *Charter for Foundation Members, 2023*.
3. Stéphanie Thomson, "'It's Too Easy to Insulate Yourself'—Davos Leaders Reflect on Social Divides," World Economic Forum, January 20, 2017.
4. Klaus Schwab with Peter Vanham, *Stakeholder Capitalism: A Global Economy That Works for Progress, People and Planet* (New Jersey: Wiley, 2021).

their workers and communities because they know it is the only way to be successful over the long term. These modernized principles reflect the business community's unwavering commitment to continue to push for an economy that serves all Americans."[1]

At the December 2019 WEF meeting, the Forum received Schwab's "Davos Manifesto 2020: The Universal Purpose of a Company in the Fourth Industrial Revolution," which expressed his vision of a company's responsibilities, including support for fair competition and a level playing field, zero tolerance for corruption, treatment of its suppliers as true partners in value creation, and respect for human rights throughout the entire supply chain.[2] A responsible company, Schwab wrote, "serves society at large through its activities, supports the communities in which it works, and pays its fair share of taxes. . . . It acts as a steward of the environmental and material universe for future generations." Asserting that "a company is more than an economic unit generating wealth," Schwab called for corporate performance "measured not only on the return to shareholders, but also on how it achieves its environmental, social and good governance objectives."[3]

Schwab's "Davos Manifesto" provides the Titans with a moral justification for continuing their path of wealth inequality while posturing as sensitive to human rights and environmental concerns. In a way, the WEF is attempting to offer salvation for capitalism's sins of starvation, war, and environmental destruction. Examining the alleged principles of that capitalist salvation and the Titans' supposed adoption of them is one important aspect of this study.

1. See Klaus Schwab and Thierry Malleret, *The Great Narrative for a Better Future* (Geneva: Forum Publishing, 2022), 109.
2. Klaus Schwab, "Davos Manifesto 2020: The Universal Purpose of a Company in the Fourth Industrial Revolution," World Economic Forum, December 2, 2019.
3. Schwab, "Davos Manifesto 2020."

The 2022 WEF sessions included addresses from top national leaders including Xi Jinping, president of the People's Republic of China; Narendra Modi, prime minister of India; Naftali Bennett, then prime minister of Israel; Fumio Kishida, prime minister of Japan; Joko Widodo, then president of Indonesia; Ursula von der Leyen, president of the European Commission; Scott Morrison, then prime minister of Australia; Yemi Osinbajo, then the acting vice president of Nigeria; and Janet Yellen, secretary of the treasury for the United States.[1]

The theme for the 2023 Davos meetings was "Cooperation in a Fragmented World." The WEF has begun using the term *polycrisis* to expand on the importance of private interests making efforts to address continuing global risks. The risks addressed during the sessions included the danger of a global recession as a result of the energy crisis emerging from the war in Ukraine, an inflation crisis impacting the cost of living for working people, and the existential threat of the global warming crisis, including extreme weather events, acidified oceans, melting arctic ice and permafrost, and increasing global forest fires. Also, in relation to the WEF's concept of polycrisis were sessions on cybercrime, "geo-economic confrontation," and "erosion of societal cohesion."[2]

The speakers at the 2023 WEF meetings included von der Leyen; Olena Zelenska, first lady of Ukraine; Liu He, then the vice premier of the People's Republic of China; Sanna Marin, then the prime minister of Finland; Pedro Sánchez, prime minister of Spain; Aziz Akhannouch, prime minister of Morocco;

---

1. "Highlight Sessions," World Economic Forum Annual Meeting (2022), World Economic Forum, accessed August 28, 2023.
2. Grace Blakeley, "At Davos, Capitalists Are Trying to Solve the Problems They Themselves Create," *Jacobin*, January 17, 2023.

Olaf Scholz, chancellor of Germany; and Yoon Suk Yeol, president of the Republic of Korea.[1]

TITANS AT THE WORLD ECONOMIC FORUM AND FIRST NOTED DATE OF PARTICIPATION (n=76)

BLACKROCK

Eleven WEF attendees out of seventeen board members (65 percent)

Laurence (Larry) D. Fink, WEF trustee, 2019, and Davos, 2015–2023; Bader M. Alsaad, 2008; Pamela Daley, Business Council WEF, 2014; Beth Ford, 2018; William E. Ford, Business Council WEF, 2012; Kristin Peck, 2022; Charles H. Robbins, 2014; Marco Antonio Slim Domit, 2012; Hans E. Vestberg, 2015; Susan Lynne Wagner, 2017, Mark Wilson, 2019

VANGUARD GROUP

Eleven WEF attendees out of eleven board members (100 percent)

Mortimer (Tim) J. Buckley, 2016; Tara Bunch, 2015; Emerson U. Fullwood, 2013; F. Joseph Loughrey, 2019; Mark Loughridge, 2013; Scott C. Malpass, 2013; Deanna Mulligan, 2018; André F. Perold, 2010; Sarah Bloom Raskin, 2017; David Thomas, 2010; Peter F. Volanakis, 2013

---

1. "Highlight Sessions," World Economic Forum Annual Meeting (2023), World Economic Forum, accessed August 28, 2023.

MORGAN STANLEY
Twelve WEF attendees out of fourteen board members (85 percent)

James P. Gorman, 2010; Alistair Darling, 2010; Thomas H. Glocer, 2010; Robert H. Herz, 2001; Erika H. James, 2017; Hironori Kamezawa, 2021; Shelley B. Leibowitz, 2020; Stephen J. Luczo, 2012; Masato Miyachi, 2022; Dennis M. Nally, 2014; Mary L. Schapiro, 2014; Perry M. Traquina, 2017

STATE STREET
Seven WEF attendees out of thirteen board members (53 percent)

Ronald P. O'Hanley, 2023; Dame Amelia C. Fawcett, 2017; Marie A. Chandoha, 2017; DonnaLee (Donna) DeMaio, 2011; Sara Mathew, 2022; William L. Meaney, 2009; Julio A. Portalatin, 2016

UBS
Eleven WEF attendees out of twelve board members (92 percent)

Colm Kelleher, 2023; Jeremy Anderson, 2020; Claudia Böckstiegel, 2021; William C. Dudley, 2015; Patrick Firmenich, 2019; Fred Hu, 2003; Mark Hughes, 2017; Nathalie Rachou, 2016; Julie G. Richardson, 2019; Dieter Wemmer, 2011; Jeanette Wong, 2016

JPMORGAN CHASE
Eight WEF attendees out of eleven board members (73 percent)

Linda B. Bammann, 2014; Jamie Dimon, 2020; Timothy P. Flynn, 2013; Alex Gorsky, 2018; Mellody Hobson, 2021; Michael A. Neal, 2015; Phebe N. Novakovic, 2022; Virginia M. Rometty, 2004

ALLIANZ GROUP
Eight WEF attendees out of eleven board members (73 percent)

Oliver Bäte, 2020; Sergio Balbinot, 2014; Sirma Boshnakova, 2014; Barbara Karuth-Zelle, 2023; Giulio Terzariol, 2020; Günther Thallinger, 2023; Renate Wagner, 2022; Andreas Wimmer, 2021

AMUNDI
Three WEF attendees out fifteen board members (20 percent)

Valérie Baudson, 2019; Yves Perrier, 2020; Philippe Brassac, 2016

CAPITAL GROUP
Zero WEF attendees out of eleven board members[1]

FIDELITY INVESTMENTS
Two WEF attendees out of three board members (67 percent)

Abigail Pierrepont Johnson, 2021; Vicki L. Fuller, 2021[2]

What is attracting 65 percent of the Titans to the WEF?

---

1. Capital Group's board of directors is made up of senior employees, often with twenty to thirty years of experience with the firm. This makes their board somewhat more provincial as compared to the other top investment management companies, where board members are often selected from outside the company based on special skills or large holdings ready for investment. This might be why Capital Group's board members are yet to participate in Davos. Nonetheless, Capital's board is still responsible for $2.7 trillion of capital investment funds and part of the Titans of Capital on the world stage.
2. It should be noted that the eleventh-largest asset management firm is Goldman Sachs. Goldman Sachs was represented by five individuals at the 2023 WEF meeting, including Jared Cohen, president of global affairs; Jim Esposito, cohead of global banking and markets; Dina Powell McCormick, global head of sovereign business; David M. Solomon, chairman and CEO; and John F. W. Rogers, executive vice president.

What are the main ideas and philosophical understandings that the WEF offers, and why are so many Titans and other global elites increasingly active at Davos and other WEF events?

Two recurring themes at the Davos meetings are the continuing need for positive economic growth and the unrestricted flow of capital investments worldwide. The main problem underlying what the WEF characterizes as a "polycrisis" is the continuing threat of economic stagnation and socioeconomic instability. The Titans realize that stagnation means declining economic growth, with corresponding damage to stock prices and corporate profits. For these reasons, in recent years the Titans have been increasingly active within the WEF. They are well aware that "polycrisis" issues threaten the stability of global capitalism. Their goal is to continue capital growth and economic wealth concentration while using the WEF as a mechanism to mediate environmental and socioeconomic threats on an international level.

The Titans and other global power elites know that they exist as a minority relative to the great majority of impoverished humanity. Roughly 80 percent of the world's population lives on less than $10 a day, while half live on less than $3.00 a day. Around seven hundred million people are victims of extreme poverty, meaning they live on $2.15 or less per person per day. Concentrated global capital becomes the binding institutional alignment that brings transnational capitalists into a centralized global imperialism. The WEF is seeking to mediate in various ways the crises brought on by concentrated capitalism while attempting to keep capitalism safely intact.[1]

In 2004 a UN report called for greater efforts by financial institutions to incorporate "environmental, social, and gover-

---

1. Credit Suisse, *Global Wealth Databook 2022.*

nance" (ESG) factors into research and planning for investment decision-making.[1] This report identified climate change and toxic releases and waste as environmental issues; workplace health and safety, community relations, and human rights in workplaces as social issues; and board accountability, executive compensation, and corruption as corporate governance issues.[2]

The WEF has long featured discussions, workshops, and reports on climate change. In 2015, for example, it produced a statement on the future of the environment titled "These 79 CEOs Believe in Global Climate Action," which asserted that "the private sector has a responsibility to engage actively in global efforts to reduce greenhouse gas emissions, and to help the world move to a low-carbon, climate-resilient economy."[3] The CEOs signing the statement included the leaders of Dow, Microsoft, Pepsi, and Accenture. The only wealth-management companies whose CEOs signed the statement were Allianz, HSBC, and UBS, which are based in Europe.

ESG funds made up approximately 31 percent of investments among professionally managed assets in 2014. This ratio is on track to rise to over 50 percent in 2024, meaning that ESG investments became increasingly popular among investors over the past decade.[4]

In late 2017 Goldman Sachs created its International Equity ESG Fund, which claimed to avoid investments in companies that derived significant revenues from gambling, adult enter-

1. United Nations Global Compact, *Who Cares Wins: Connecting Financial Markets to a Changing World* (United Nations, 2004).
2. Ibid.
3. Alliance of CEO Climate Leaders, "These 79 CEOs Believe in Global Climate Action," World Economic Forum, November 23, 2015.
4. Tania Lynn Taylor and Sean Collins, "Ingraining Sustainability in the Next Era of ESG Investing," *Deloitte Insights*, April 5, 2022.

tainment, alcohol, tobacco, coal, and weapons.[1] Since then more than ninety mutual funds and exchange-traded funds (ETFs) that claim to be ESG-sensitive have been created. BlackRock, JPMorgan Chase, Morgan Stanley, and others have joined in offering ESG investment funds. The Securities and Exchange Commission has been reviewing the ESG offerings for truth in advertising.[2]

Currently, all the top ten largest investment management firms claim to be ESG-sensitive and offer varying investment opportunities that comply with some form of ESG standards. Even Capital Group has joined in the ESG policy position, having reported in 2021 that "global investors strongly prefer an active approach to ESG."[3]

The WEF has encouraged the building of common metrics for evaluating sustainability and ESG in the hopes of diminishing the negative impacts of concentrated wealth on the environment and social justice. Stakeholder capitalism is viewed by the WEF as the panacea for saving capitalism from itself. "New case studies from the World Economic Forum show how comprehensive environmental, social and corporate governance (ESG) reporting has started to drive corporate transformation around the world, particularly in sustainability efforts and company culture," the WEF asserted in a 2022 press release.[4]

ESG has been incorporated into the curricula of the top business programs at the most prestigious academic institutions. The business schools of Harvard, Yale, and the University of Pennsylvania all offer courses that evaluate ESG standards. In

---

1. Goldman Sachs, *Goldman Sachs Focused International Equity Fund*, December 15, 2017.
2. Matthew Goldstein and Emily Flitter, "Cracking Down on a Wall Street Trend: E.S.G. Makeovers," *New York Times*, September 17, 2022.
3. Capital Group, *ESG Global Study 2021* (Capital International Management Company, 2021).
4. Madeleine Hillyer, "Commitment to ESG Reporting Is Driving Change within Global Corporations, New Study Shows," World Economic Forum, press release, September 22, 2022.

2022 the *New York Times* reported that "nearly half" of the Yale School of Management's curriculum is devoted to ESG, while Harvard Business School offers a course, "Reimagining Capitalism," in which students consider how corporations address their obligations to society.[1]

Even the Vatican has called for ethical investment practices. In November 2022, Cardinal Peter Turkson released a guide to the best practices for ethical investing that steers Catholic investment management to comply with the social doctrine of the Church. The Catholic Church is supposed to set investment priorities that protect the environment and immigrants and avoid investments in gambling, polluters, war profiteers, adult entertainment, or tax havens that use loopholes to avoid fair taxes.[2]

Standards for ESG are highly debated and increasingly challenged. One of the original—and most contested—ESG issues is climate change. Widespread news reports on global warming, melting glaciers, rising oceans, and extreme weather have created broad anxieties about Earth's future habitability. In its *Climate Change 2023* report, the Intergovernmental Panel on Climate Change noted:

> Finance, international cooperation and technology are critical enablers for accelerated climate action. If climate goals are to be achieved, both adaptation and mitigation financing would have to increase many-fold. There is sufficient global capital to close the global investment gaps but there are barriers to redirect capital to climate action.

1. Emma Goldberg, "Have the Anticapitalists Reached Harvard Business School?," *New York Times*, November 28, 2022.

2. Jason Horowitz, "Catholic Church Issues Guidelines for Ethical Investing," *New York Times*, November 25, 2022.

The IPCC report went on to note that these barriers include "institutional, regulatory and market access barriers."[1]

Many claim that ESG practices should include a standard report on a business organization's carbon footprint, natural resources used, waste management, and climate impacts. However, making strong ESG modifications to a company's business practices can be costly and—in the cases of fossil fuel companies, arms manufacturers, pharmaceutical firms, junk food franchises, cigarette makers, and many others—can undermine the profitability of the companies and certainly challenge the ESG values of all major capital investment firms.

Despite ESG and concern for the environment, global inequality, monetary crises, civil unrest, and threats of world war—any of which could hinder economic growth and returns on investments—the most important issues for both the WEF and the Titans remain firm: protecting capital investment, ensuring debt collection, and building opportunities for further returns. The WEF serves as a constant reminder for the Titans to remain vigilant and aware of the continuing polycrisis and its threats to the stability of global wealth investment and consolidation.

In 2017 BlackRock and Vanguard—which together hold 13 percent of the shares in ExxonMobil, worth approximately $43.6 billion—joined a significant number of ExxonMobil shareholders to pass a nonbinding recommendation that the company attempt to hold global temperature changes to two degrees Celsius, the goal established by the 2015 Paris Agreement. BlackRock and Vanguard shareholders were concerned with long-term stock price viability and wanted ExxonMobil to study possible ESG

1. Intergovernmental Panel on Climate Change (IPCC), "Sections," in *Climate Change 2023: Synthesis Report*. Contribution of Working Groups I, II and III to the Sixth Assessment Report of the Intergovernmental Panel on Climate Change, eds. H. Lee and J. Romero (Geneva, Switzerland: IPCC, 2023), III.

impacts on profitability.[1] ExxonMobil claims to be ESG sensitive. According to its website, the company "remains determined to tackle head-on the challenges of strengthening energy supply security and reducing emissions to support a net-zero future while growing value for our shareholders and stakeholders."[2]

ExxonMobil's annual revenue was $264 billion in 2019 and $413 billion in 2022, a 69 percent increase in sales over three years. At the same time, both BlackRock and Vanguard have more than doubled the value of their investments in the company.

BlackRock	ExxonMobil shares	$23.1 billion (2023)
Vanguard	ExxonMobil shares	$72.4 billion (2023)
	Total:	$95.5 billion

New research has shown that, dating back more than four decades, ExxonMobil's own studies accurately predicted that burning fossil fuels would result in global warming at 0.20 degrees centigrade per decade. Yet executives at ExxonMobil suppressed its own scientific findings. The coverup of that research is part of a larger strategy employed by ExxonMobil to deny the consequences of fossil fuel use in climate change by overemphasizing uncertainties, denigrating climate models, and mythologizing global warming.[3]

How multinational corporations such as ExxonMobil can claim to be ESG sensitive while simultaneously massively increasing oil and gas sales is difficult to comprehend. At the same time, ESG policies promoted by capital investment man-

1. Diane Cardwell, "Exxon Mobil Shareholders Demand Accounting of Climate Change Policy Risks," *New York Times*, May 31, 2017.

2. "2023 Advancing Climate Solutions Progress Report," ExxonMobil, accessed August 28, 2023.

3. Sharon Zhang, "Study Reveals Exxon Accurately Predicted Global Warming Decades Ago," Truthout, January 12, 2023.

agement companies and other major corporations with global impacts are under attack. Republican-controlled state and local governments in the United States are threatening lawsuits against investment companies for using ESG standards, asserting that government regulations implement "woke" policies at the expense of shareholder profits. Texas attorney general Ken Paxton claimed that ESG climate goals hurt Texas's oil and gas economy and impacted the performance of the state's pension fund. Texas claims that the companies engaging in such practices are in violation of their fiduciary responsibility to maximize returns for their shareholders. In August 2022, the state of Texas joined a coalition of eighteen other Republican-led states that criticized BlackRock's ESG policy for reducing shareholder profits in state pension funds.[1]

BlackRock CEO Larry Fink responded that the company's critics "have their facts wrong. BlackRock sees climate change as a risk, but we are not boycotting oil and gas companies." In January 2023, at the World Economic Forum in Davos, Fink stated, "We are trying to address the misconceptions. Unfortunately, there are some politicians who are taking some parts of a sentence out of context." In a later written statement on ESG, Fink said, "We manage money on behalf of our clients to help them . . . achieve their financial goals."[2]

Despite each of the top ten capital investment companies managed by the Titans claiming to hold an ESG policy, collective investment in the top nine oil and gas firms contributing to global warming continues at significant levels.

---

1. Jose Nino, "Texas Is the Latest State to Join 18 Other States to Stand Up against Blackrock's Woke Policies," *Big League Politics*, August 13, 2022.

2. Scott Tong, Jill Ryan, and Catherine Welch, "Audio Recording Reveals Coordinated Push against ESG Investing," *Here & Now*, WBUR (Boston, MA), March 22, 2023.

EXXONMOBIL, US

2022 REVENUE: $386.8 billion

INSTITUTIONAL OWNERS (total number of investor entities): 4,840

Titan investors:

Vanguard	$72.4 billion
State Street	$29.1 billion
BlackRock	$23.1 billion
Fidelity Investments	$20.2 billion
Capital	$6.4 billion
Morgan Stanley	$5.7 billion
JPMorgan Chase	$4.1 billion
Amundi	$2.3 billion
UBS	$1.9 billion
Allianz/PIMCO	$470 million

Total Titan investment	$165.7 billion

CHEVRON CORPORATION, US

2022 REVENUE: $227.1 billion

INSTITUTIONAL OWNERS: 4,558

Titan investors:

Vanguard	$41.8 billion
State Street	$32 billion
BlackRock	$24.2 billion
Morgan Stanley	$7.5 billion
Capital	$5.7 billion
JPMorgan Chase	$2.97 billion
Fidelity Investments	$2.7 billion
UBS	$1.9 billion
Amundi	$1.7 billion
Allianz/PIMCO	$232 million

Total Titan investment	$120.7 billion

CONOCOPHILLIPS, US
2022 REVENUE: $82.156 billion

INSTITUTIONAL OWNERS: 3,390

Titan investors:

Vanguard	$20.04 billion
BlackRock	$13.2 billion
State Street	$7.4 billion
Capital	$6.7 billion
JPMorgan Chase	$5.7 billion
Fidelity Investments	$5.2 billion
Morgan Stanley	$1.7 billion
UBS	$762 million
Amundi	$381 million
Allianz/PIMCO	$127 million
Total Titan investment	$61.21 billion

PHILLIPS 66, US
2022 REVENUE: $169.99 billion

INSTITUTIONAL OWNERS: 2,484

Titan investors:

Vanguard	$8.23 billion
State Street	$5 billion
BlackRock	$3.55 billion
Fidelity Investments	$1.17 billion
Morgan Stanley	$645 million
UBS	$353 million
JPMorgan Chase	$330 million
Amundi	$251 million
Allianz/PIMCO	$208 million
Capital	$41.4 million
Total Titan investment	$20.15 billion

MARATHON PETROLEUM CORPORATION, US
2022 REVENUE: $173 billion
INSTITUTIONAL OWNERS: 2,387

Titan investors:

Vanguard	$5.1 billion
BlackRock	$5.1 billion
State Street	$3.45 billion
Morgan Stanley	$914 million
Capital	$707 million
Fidelity Investments	$636 million
UBS	$635 million
Amundi	$584 million
Allianz/PIMCO	$284 million
JPMorgan Chase	$130 million
Total Titan investment	$17.54 billion

VALERO ENERGY CORPORATION, US
2022 REVENUE: $170.5 billion
INSTITUTIONAL OWNERS: 54

Titan investors:

Vanguard	$5.3 billion
BlackRock	$3.5 billion
Fidelity Investments	$1.9 billion
Morgan Stanley	$641 million
UBS	$468 million
Capital	$415 million
Amundi	$414 million
Allianz/PIMCO	$348 million
JPMorgan Chase	$217 million
Total Titan investment	$13.2 billion

BP, UK

2022 REVENUE: $222.7 billion

INSTITUTIONAL OWNERS: 488

Titan investors:

BlackRock	$1.2 billion
State Street	$851 million
Vanguard	$776 million
Morgan Stanley	$475.5 million
UBS	$239 million
Fidelity Investments	$113.3 million
Capital	$108.6 million
JPMorgan Chase	$102 million
Amundi	$12.6 million

Total Titan investment	$3.87 billion

SHELL, UK

2022 REVENUE: $365.3 billion

INSTITUTIONAL OWNERS: 1,409

Titan investors:

Fidelity Investments	$1.2 billion
BlackRock	$558 million
Morgan Stanley	$541 million
Vanguard	$521 million
Amundi	$199 million
State Street	$128 million
JPMorgan Chase	$118 million
Capital	$114 million
UBS	$109 million

Total Titan investment	$3.488 billion

TOTALENERGIES, FRANCE

2022 REVENUE: $254.7 billion

INSTITUTIONAL OWNERS: 825

Titan investors:

Fidelity Investments	$1.2 billion
Morgan Stanley	$402.9 million
Vanguard	$377.2 million
Amundi	$350 million
Capital	$348.1 million
BlackRock	$347.3 million
JPMorgan Chase	$168.4 million
UBS	$22 million
Total Titan investment	$3.21 billion

In sum, Titan investments in fossil fuel companies based in the US, UK, and France total more than $409 billion. Three of the Titans also invest in Saudi Aramco, otherwise known as the Saudi Arabian Oil Group—the world's second-largest oil company by 2022 revenues—which is jointly held by the government of Saudi Arabia (a 90 percent share) and Saudi Arabia's Public Investment Fund (10 percent).

SAUDI ARAMCO

2022 REVENUE: $590.3 billion

Titan investors:

Vanguard	$763.8 million
BlackRock	$557.4 million
Fidelity Investments	$67.9 million
Total Titan investment	$1.38 billion

In February 2023, CBS News reported that global oil companies posted their "highest ever profits" in 2022. ConocoPhillips, Chevron, Exxon, and Shell boasted combined sales of more than $1 trillion, CBS reported, noting that record profits followed "a year of skyrocketing gas prices" and the Russian invasion of Ukraine, which "shrank the world's oil supplies, bringing the average price of gas in the US above $5 a gallon in the spring and summer."[1]

Investors claim progress toward net-zero emissions by putting money into the carbon credit market. JPMorgan Chase paid $1 million to "preserve forestland in eastern Pennsylvania" that was never threatened, as the trees were already part of a well-preserved forest. BlackRock did the same by paying the city of Albany to refrain from cutting trees around its reservoirs.[2] Carbon-offset credits allow a company to continue investing heavily in global warming gases by offsetting those investments with "protection" of forests. But as Project Censored has highlighted—based on original reporting from the *Guardian*, *Die Zeit*, and SourceMaterial—the carbon-offset industry is unregulated and rife with conflicts of interest, with independent studies determining that up to 90 percent of rainforest carbon offsets verified by Verra, the world's largest offset certifier, are "worthless" and do not reflect real reductions in emissions.[3]

Global climate change continues to be a serious issue for people worldwide. In France, in May 2023, more than seven hundred activists from climate-protection advocacy groups

---

1. Irina Ivanova, "4 Oil Companies Had Total Sales of $1 Trillion Last Year," CBS News, February 2, 2023.

2. Ben Elgin, "These Trees Are Not What They Seem," *Bloomberg*, December 9, 2020.

3. See Annie Koruga and Mickey Huff, "Certified Rainforest Carbon Offsets Mostly 'Worthless,'" in *State of the Free Press 2024*, eds. Andy Lee Roth and Mickey Huff (Fair Oaks, CA and New York: The Censored Press and Seven Stories Press, 2024), 37–41.

protested outside the Salle Pleyel, where TotalEnergies was holding its annual shareholder meeting. The company had just reported a 2022 net profit of $36.2 billion. Stating that fossil fuel companies have no future unless they switch to renewable energy, activists from 350.org, Greenpeace, Friends of the Earth, and Scientist Rebellion called on TotalEnergies to cut its emissions by half. Police met the demonstrators with tear gas, pepper spray, and arrests.[1] Titans, led by Fidelity Investments, have a combined $3.21 billion invested in TotalEnergies.

COAL AND GLOBAL WARMING

Burning coal produces the highest carbon emissions, and more than eight billion tons were burned in 2022.[2] The International Energy Agency (IEA) predicts that, after peaking in 2022, coal consumption will "remain flat at that level through 2025."[3] The IEA estimates that there are nine thousand coal-fired power plants in the world today, noting that clean energy alternatives to coal will require "massive financing."[4] For now, however, Titans remain heavily invested in the world's largest coal-mining companies, as detailed in the following list, based on 2022 investment figures.

1. Julia Conley, "French Protest 'Climate-Wrecking Projects and Massive Profits' of TotalEnergies," Common Dreams, May 26, 2023.
2. "The World's Coal Consumption Is Set to Reach a New High in 2022 as the Energy Crisis Shakes Markets," International Energy Agency, December 16, 2022.
3. "World's Coal."
4. "Achieving a Swift Reduction in Global Coal Emissions Is the Central Challenge for Reaching International Climate Targets," International Energy Agency, November 15, 2022.

BHP GROUP, AUSTRALIA
2022 REVENUE: $60.8 billion
INSTITUTIONAL OWNERS: 1,248

Titan investors:

Vanguard	$2.42 billion
BlackRock	$1.58 billion
State Street	$1.41 billion
JPMorgan Chase	$828 million
Amundi	$230 million
Allianz/PIMCO	$16 million
Total Titan investment	$6.51 billion

RIO TINTO, AUSTRALIA
2022 REVENUE: $50.5 billion
INSTITUTIONAL OWNERS: 1,327

Titan investors:

BlackRock	$1.2 billion
Vanguard	$834 million
Capital	$540 million
Morgan Stanley	$236 million
Fidelity Investments	$175 million
UBS	$50 million
JPMorgan Chase	$18 million
Amundi	$6.5 million
Total Titan investment	$3.06 billion

ANGLO AMERICAN, UK
2022 REVENUE: $35.7 billion[1]
INSTITUTIONAL OWNERS: 582

Titan investors:

Vanguard	$1.29 billion
BlackRock	$582 million
Fidelity Investments	$306 million
JPMorgan Chase	$112 million
State Street	$63.2 million
Allianz/PIMCO	$5.2 million
Total Titan investment	$2.35 billion

CHINA SHENHUA ENERGY, CHINA
2022 REVENUE: $50.4 billion[2]
INSTITUTIONAL OWNERS: 205

Titan investors:

BlackRock	$484 million
Vanguard	$451 million
State Street	$146.5 million
Morgan Stanley	$2 million
Total Titan investment	$1.08 billion

The Titans are also invested in the largest US-based coal-mining companies. 2022 investment figures for coal:

---

1. Anglo American reported 14.8 million tons of CO_2 emissions in 2021.
2. Shenhua reported 134 million tons of CO_2 emissions in 2020.

PEABODY ENERGY, US
2022 REVENUE: $4.9 billion
INSTITUTIONAL OWNERS: 513

Titan investors:

Vanguard	$229 million
BlackRock	$148 million
State Street	$115 million
Capital	$24 million
Morgan Stanley	$22 million
JPMorgan Chase	$13 million
UBS	$3.2 million
Total Titan investment	$554.2 million

ARCH RESOURCES, US
2022 REVENUE: $3.7 billion
INSTITUTIONAL OWNERS: 472

Titan investors:

Vanguard	$206 million
BlackRock	$111 million
State Street	$102 million
Fidelity Investments	$93 million
Morgan Stanley	$75 million
JPMorgan Chase	$19 million
UBS	$2.1 million
Allianz/PIMCO	$380,000
Total Titan investment	$606.4 million

Overall, Titan investments in the largest coal-mining companies totaled more than $14 billion in 2022.

Natural gas is often cited as a better energy source than oil or coal because its combustion releases about half as many carbon emissions as coal and 30 percent less than oil. However, producing natural gas involves the release of methane, which the Center for Climate and Energy Solutions notes "has a global warming potential 21 times higher than carbon dioxide over a 100-year period."[1]

In 2021, the largest producers of natural gas included the following companies:

Company	Revenue, in billions (2021)
Gazprom (Russia)	$137
PetroChina	$366
Sinopec (China)	$383
ExxonMobil (US)	$285
Shell (UK)	$272
BP (UK)	$164
Chevron (US)	$155
TotalEnergies (France)	$205
Rosneft (Russia)	$122
Lukoil (Russia)	$131

The war in Ukraine has limited Russia's ability to sell natural gas to Europe. Sanctions on Russia have opened up vast new opportunities for the major oil companies to expand sales of natural gas in Europe with increasing dividends to Titan investors.

Efforts by the Titans to claim they support ESG factors and care about addressing the threat of global warming are contradicted by their deep, continued investments in companies that profit from the extraction of oil, coal, and natural gas and thus contribute significantly to the world's unsustainable levels of carbon emissions. It is important to note that the Titans are

---

1. "Natural Gas," Climate Solutions, Technology Solutions, Center for Climate and Energy Solutions, accessed August 28, 2023.

playing a global leadership role through their capital-investment decisions. They choose to continue pursuing profitable investments in fossil fuels despite the very real threat of climate devastation on a global scale.

In a blatant effort to control CO_2 levels without reducing emissions, the World Economic Forum has promoted direct air capture since 2020. That year, the forum lauded Climeworks, based in Switzerland, and Carbon Engineering, in Canada, as two of its "Technology Pioneers" that are working to develop tools to capture carbon dioxide from the air, reducing CO_2 levels before releasing it back into the atmosphere.[1]

In 2023, the Biden administration approved $1.2 billion in Department of Energy funding to build two direct air capture plants in the United States. In reporting the development, the *New York Times* noted that environmentalists have criticized direct air capture as "an extravagant boondoggle."[2] For example, Al Gore described the direct air capture technology as a "moral hazard" that will enable fossil fuel producers to continue to pollute.

A Texas-based company, Occidental Petroleum—in which the Titans have $12.8 billion invested—is slated to build one of the plants; the other will be built by Battelle Memorial Institute, a nonprofit research group based in Ohio. The *Times* reported that the US government would eventually develop two additional direct air capture plants, drawing on $3.5 billion allocated for the project in the 2021 bipartisan infrastructure law.[3]

Battelle is highly connected with the Pentagon and US

---

1. Joe Myers, "These 2 Companies Can Pull CO_2 Straight from the Air," World Economic Forum, June 26, 2020.
2. Coral Davenport, "U.S. to Fund a $1.2 Billion Effort to Vacuum Greenhouse Gases from the Sky," *New York Times*, August 11, 2023.
3. Davenport, "U.S. to Fund a $1.2 Billion Effort."

intelligence agencies. It manages or co-manages nine national nuclear and biodefense labs, including the Los Alamos, Lawrence Livermore, and Savannah River labs.[1] Board chair Kirkland H. Donald is a retired Navy admiral and former director of the Naval Nuclear Propulsion Program. Stephanie O'Sullivan, who has served as the principal deputy director of national intelligence and a senior leader at the CIA, is also a member of Battelle's board of directors, along with Suzanne M. Vautrinot, a former major general in the US Air Force and commander of its Air Force Cyber Command.

This brings into question the ESG claims of oil companies and their Titan investors. Have they ever intended to cut back on the releases of global warming gases, or are they counting on a technological intervention? The Titans' decisions to continue making enormous investments in companies responsible for the climate crisis pose threats to the entire world.

A 2023 study produced by an international team of scientists and published in *Nature* magazine concluded that "seven of the eight globally quantified ESBs [Earth system boundaries] have been crossed . . . putting human livelihoods for current and future generations at risk."[2] Based on this data, the study's authors contended that "a safe and just future" would require "a leap in our understanding of how justice, economics, technology and global cooperation can be furthered." An Associated Press report on the study quoted its lead author, Johan Rockström, who said, "We are moving in the wrong direction" in our current use of coal, oil, and natural gas.[3] "The planet is nearing the edge of boundaries that would launch us into

1. "National Laboratory Management and Operations," Battelle, accessed August 30, 2023.
2. Johan Rockström et al., "Safe and Just Earth System Boundaries," *Nature* 619 (2023).
3. Seth Borenstein, "Earth Is 'Really Quite Sick Now' and in Danger Zone in Nearly All Ecological Ways, Study Says," Associated Press, May 31, 2023.

irreversible states," Indy Burke, dean of the Yale School of the Environment, told the AP.

The *Nature* study followed the publication, in January 2023, of a report in *Advances in Atmospheric Sciences*, which found that 2022 was another year of record ocean temperatures. The world's oceans "were again the hottest in the historical record and exceeded the previous 2021 record maximum," Lijing Cheng and a joint team of US and Chinese scientists reported.[1] Changes in Earth's energy and water cycles have been "profoundly altered" by greenhouse gas emissions resulting from human activity, they reported.

In a vicious cycle, as climate change contributes to more frequent and intense heat waves, the demand for fossil fuels may actually increase. As Eco-Business reported in May 2023, demand for electricity across South and Southeast Asia spiked significantly when temperatures in the region exceeded 113 degrees Fahrenheit (45 degrees Celsius) for several weeks in spring 2023, with countries including India, Malaysia, and Thailand facing "record-breaking power demand as people turn[ed] to air conditioning en masse."[2] "Because of the heatwave . . . countries in the region may turn to coal more aggressively than ever," Victor Nian, chief executive of a Singapore think tank, the Centre for Strategic Energy and Resources, told Eco-Business.

Widespread calls for immediate action in response to the climate crisis are emerging worldwide. But not everyone is assured by corporate pledges of climate action. In April 2022, for example, UN secretary general António Guterres stated, "Some government and business leaders are saying one thing,

---

1. Lijing Cheng et al., "Another Year of Record Heat for the Oceans," *Advances in Atmospheric Sciences* 40 (2023).
2. Liang Lei, "As Asian Heatwaves Require Burning More Fossil Fuels, Fears of a Slower Transition Grow," Eco-Business, May, 31, 2023.

but doing another. Simply put, they are lying."[1] And in Peter Gelderloos's 2022 book, *The Solutions Are Already Here: Strategies for Ecological Revolution from Below*, the activist and writer calls for a bottom-up ecosystem revolt by activists resisting "ecocide."[2] "This is still a battle that pits David against Goliath," Gelderloos writes.[3] It is exceedingly clear that the Titans are among the Goliaths in today's precarious world.

1. Damian Carrington, "It's Over for Fossil Fuels: IPCC Spells Out What's Needed to Avert Climate Disaster," *The Guardian*, April 4, 2022.

2. Peter Gelderloos, *The Solutions Are Already Here: Strategies for Ecological Revolution from Below* (London: Pluto Press, 2022).

3. Gelderloos, *Solutions*, 206; see also Ella Fassler, "We Are Running Out of Time to Use Failing Strategies against the Climate Crisis," Truthout, November 24, 2022.

CHAPTER 4

TITANS IN SOCIALLY HARMFUL INVESTMENTS
Tobacco, Alcohol, Plastics, Firearms, Gambling, and Private Prisons

The *S* in ESG stands for *social impacts* that affect people's health, safety, equality, civil rights, and labor rights. Investments that negatively affect society are an important aspect of ESG practices. Titans like to proclaim a consciousness of social issues; however, their investment decisions tell a different story.

TOBACCO ABUSE

More than 250 billion cigarettes were sold in the United States in 2022. Noting that smoking causes cancer, heart disease, strokes, lung disease, diabetes, and chronic obstructive pulmonary disease (including emphysema and chronic bronchitis), the Centers for Disease Control and Prevention have stated, "More than 16 million Americans are living with a disease caused by smoking" and that, for each person who dies because of smoking, "at least 30 people live with a serious smoking-related illness."[1]

The World Health Organization reports that over 8 mil-

---

1. "Smoking & Tobacco Use: Health Effects," Centers for Disease Control and Prevention, last updated April 28, 2020.

lion people die annually from smoking, including 1.3 million nonsmokers who die from secondhand exposure.[1] Despite the harms of tobacco use, Titans are heavily invested in the world's largest tobacco companies, as indicated by the Titan holdings in the following six companies.

TITAN INVESTMENTS IN WORLD'S LARGEST TOBACCO COMPANIES

CHINA NATIONAL TOBACCO CORPORATION, BEIJING

2022 REVENUE: $273 billion

INSTITUTIONAL OWNERS: 90 percent government owned

CHINA NATIONAL TOBACCO CORPORATION, HONG KONG

2022 REVENUE: $1.05 billion

INSTITUTIONAL OWNERS: Subsidiary of China National Tobacco Corporation, Beijing

Titan investors in 2022:

BlackRock	$56.5 million
Vanguard	$44 million
State Street	$5.7 million
Total Titan investments:	$106.2 million

IMPERIAL BRANDS, UK

2022 REVENUE: $41.6 billion

INSTITUTIONAL OWNERS: 406

Titan investors in 2022:

BlackRock	$1.1 billion
Capital	$95 million

---

1. "Tobacco Fact Sheet," World Health Organization, July 31, 2023.

Fidelity Investments	$62.3 million
Vanguard	$59.8 million

Total Titan investments:	$1.32 billion

BRITISH AMERICAN TOBACCO, UK
2022 REVENUE: $34.2 billion
INSTITUTIONAL OWNERS: 486

Titan investors in 2022:

Capital	$1.5 billion
BlackRock	$445 million
JPMorgan Chase	$134 million
Vanguard	$78 million

Total Titan investments:	$2.16 billion

PHILIP MORRIS INTERNATIONAL, US
2022 REVENUE: $31.7 billion
INSTITUTIONAL OWNERS: 3,184

Titan investors in 2022:

Capital	$23.5 billion
Vanguard	$20.1 billion
BlackRock	$8.7 billion
State Street	$5.2 billion
Morgan Stanley	$3.9 billion
JPMorgan Chase	$2.4 billion
Fidelity Investments	$1.5 billion
UBS	$341,130
Amundi	$39,351
Allianz/PIMCO	$29,538

Total Titan investments:	$65.3 billion

ALTRIA, US
2022 REVENUE: $25 billion
INSTITUTIONAL OWNERS: 2,739

Titan investors in 2022:

Vanguard	$11.68 billion
Capital	$8.8 billion
BlackRock	$6.7 billion
State Street	$4.8 billion
Fidelity Investments	$1.13 billion
Morgan Stanley	$831 million
JPMorgan Chase	$416 million
UBS	$230 million
Allianz/PIMCO	$6.9 million
Total Titan investments:	$34.6 billion

In 2022, the Titans invested a total of $103.49 billion in the world's largest tobacco companies, making them active investors in the deaths of millions of people annually.

ALCOHOL ABUSE

The World Health Organization estimates that harmful use of alcohol results in three million deaths around the world annually and that alcohol accounts for 5.1 percent of the global burden of disease and injury.[1] Beyond injuries and fatalities resulting from traffic accidents, violence, and suicide, the health problems associated with alcohol consumption include "mental and behavioral disorders, including alcohol dependence, and major noncommunicable diseases such as liver cirrhosis, some cancers and cardiovascular diseases," according to the WHO.

---

1. "Alcohol," World Health Organization, May 9, 2022.

In 2014, the *Washington Post* reported that the top 10 percent of American adults who use alcohol consume an average of seventy-four drinks per week.[1] These twenty-four million adults "account for well over half of the alcohol consumed in any given year" in the United States, the *Post* reported. Put in terms relevant to my research, the alcoholic beverage industry profits massively from addicted consumers.

TITAN INVESTMENTS IN THE WORLD'S LARGEST LIQUOR MAKERS AND DISTRIBUTORS

DIAGEO, UK
2022 REVENUE: $28.17 billion[2]

INSTITUTIONAL OWNERS: 1,147

Titan investors in 2022:

BlackRock	$3.75 billion
Capital	$3.23 billion
Vanguard	$1.89 billion
Fidelity Investments	$936 million
Morgan Stanley	$394 million
UBS	$379 million
JPMorgan Chase	$65.5 million
State Street	$1.5 million
Allianz/PIMCO	$391,000
Amundi	$181,000
Total Titan investments:	$10.65 billion

1. Christopher Ingraham, "Think You Drink a Lot? This Chart Will Tell You," *Washington Post*, September 25, 2014.
2. Diageo operates in 180 countries around the world. Its top brands include: Johnnie Walker, Seagram's Seven Crown, Crown Royal, Smirnoff, Ketel One, Cîroc, Captain Morgan, Baileys, Don Julio, Gilbey's, Tanqueray, Guinness, Harp, and sixty others.

LVMH, FRANCE
2022 REVENUE: $79.2 billion[1]
INSTITUTIONAL INVESTORS: 102

Titan investors in 2022:

Capital	$10.3 billion
BlackRock	$6.6 billion
Vanguard	$5.8 billion
Fidelity Investments	$3.8 billion
Amundi	$2.8 billion
JPMorgan Chase	$1.1 billion

Total Titan investments:	$30.4 billion

KWEICHOW MOUTAI, CHINA
2022 REVENUE: $19.38 billion
INSTITUTIONAL INVESTORS: 283

Titan investors in 2022:

Capital	$2.4 billion
Vanguard	$585 million
UBS	$444 million
JPMorgan Chase	$350 million

Total Titan investments:	$3.7 billion

---

1. LVMH's top alcohol brands include Moët, Dom Pérignon, and Hennessy, which account for approximately $15 billion, or 18.8 percent of its revenues; the company also produces and profits from the sales of luxury leather goods, watches, jewelry, perfumes, and cosmetics.

AB INBEV, BELGIUM
2022 REVENUE: $57.78 billion
INSTITUTIONAL OWNERS: 486

Titan investors in 2022:

BlackRock	$476.5 million
Capital	$375 million
Vanguard	$226 million
Fidelity Investments	$135.1 million
Morgan Stanley	$88.8 million
Allianz/PIMCO	$45 million
JPMorgan Chase	$40 million
State Street	$11.2 million
Total Titan investments:	$1.39 billion

PERNOD RICARD USA
2022 REVENUE: $11.17 billion[1]
INSTITUTIONAL OWNERS: 492

Titan investors in 2022:

Vanguard	$1.66 billion
Fidelity Investments	$637 million
BlackRock	$404.5 million
JPMorgan Chase	$119.4 million
Morgan Stanley	$41.2 million
State Street	$18 million
Allianz/PIMCO	$4.1 million
Capital	$940,000
Total Titan investments:	$2.89 billion

---

1. Pernod Ricard USA's brands include Absolut, Glenlivet, Jameson, and Mumm.

CONSTELLATION BRANDS, US
2022 REVENUE: $8.8 billion[1]

INSTITUTIONAL OWNERS: 2,058

Titan investors in 2022:

Vanguard	$4.7 billion
State Street	$1.9 billion
BlackRock	$1.8 billion
Capital	$1.4 billion
JPMorgan Chase	$706 million
Fidelity Investments	$414 million
Total Titan investments:	$10.92 billion

In 2022, the Titans invested a total of $60.1 billion in the world's top six alcohol producers and distributors, whose products lead to the deaths of millions of people annually.

GLOBAL PLASTICS POLLUTION

The World Economic Forum is calling for a new approach to plastic pollution. It says the world needs to reverse the annual use of virgin plastics made from fossil fuels by at least 3 percent: "Plastic use is growing worldwide and is projected to almost triple by 2060."[2]

Plastics comprise 85 percent of all ocean waste, with eleven million tons entering the oceans annually. Microplastics fill the bodies of fish, marine animals, and seabirds. The US claims that plastic reduction needs to be country-based instead of a global effort, thereby delaying world action on the issue. The

---

1. Constellation Brands' portfolio includes Casa Modelo, Corona, Casa Noble, and Robert Mondavi.
2. Mark Schneider and Antoine de Saint-Affrique, "Why It's Time for a Coordinated Global Approach to Plastic Pollution," World Economic Forum, June 2, 2023.

Philippines and India currently rank highest globally in plastic pollution,[1] yet North America and China produce more than half the plastics in the world.[2] Citing reports from the *Guardian*, Truthout, the Intercept, and other independent news outlets, Project Censored has highlighted the presence of harmful microplastics in seafood, human blood, and rainwater.[3] The United Nations Environment Programme warns that "exposure to plastics can harm human health, potentially affecting fertility, hormonal, metabolic and neurological activity, and open burning of plastics contributes to air pollution."[4]

TITAN INVESTMENTS IN THE WORLD'S TOP PLASTIC MANUFACTURERS

DOW CHEMICAL COMPANY, US
2022 REVENUE: $60.2 billion

INSTITUTIONAL OWNERS: 2,803

Titan investors in 2022:

Vanguard	$5.8 billion
State Street	$2.3 billion
BlackRock	$2.1 billion

1. Christine Keating, "The US Shouldn't Stand in the Way of an Ambitious Global Plastics Treaty," Common Dreams, June 8, 2023.

2. "Distribution of Global Plastic Materials Production in 2021, by Region," Chemicals & Resources, Plastic & Rubber, Statista, December 2022.

3. See Eduardo Amador et al., "Microplastics and Toxic Chemicals Increasingly Prevalent in World's Oceans," in *State of the Free Press 2022*, eds. Andy Lee Roth and Mickey Huff (Fair Oaks, CA and New York: The Censored Press and Seven Stories Press, 2022), 49–53, accessible online in Project Censored's archive of its annual Top 25 story lists; Mark Parlatore et al., "Déjà Vu News," in *State of the Free Press 2023*, eds. Mickey Huff and Andy Lee Roth (Fair Oaks, CA and New York: The Censored Press and Seven Stories Press, 2022), 115–9; and Grace Harty and Steve Macek, "'Forever Chemicals' in Rainwater a Global Threat to Human Health," in *State of the Free Press 2024*, eds. Andy Lee Roth and Mickey Huff (Fair Oaks, CA and New York: The Censored Press and Seven Stories Press, 2023), 23–26.

4. "Historic Day in the Campaign to Beat Plastic Pollution: Nations Commit to Develop a Legally Binding Agreement," United Nations Environmental Programme, press release, March 2, 2022.

Capital	$767 million
Morgan Stanley	$510 million
JPMorgan Chase	$450 million
Fidelity Investments	$426 million
UBS	$171 million
Amundi	$151 million
Allianz/PIMCO	$36.5 million
Total Titan investments:	$12.7 billion

LYONDELLBASELL, US
2022 REVENUE: $47.54 billion

INSTITUTIONAL OWNERS: 1,724

Titan investors in 2022:

Vanguard	$5.7 billion
BlackRock	$1.96 billion
State Street	$1.1 billion
Capital	$748 million
Morgan Stanley	$485 million
Fidelity Investments	$415 million
JPMorgan Chase	$385 million
UBS	$192 million
Amundi	$41.4 million
Allianz/PIMCO	$6.7 million
Total Titan investments:	$11.03 billion

EXXONMOBIL, US
2022 REVENUE: $386.8 billion
INSTITUTIONAL OWNERS: 4,840

Note: This is the same data used for ExxonMobil in Chapter 3.

Titan investors in 2022:

Vanguard	$72.4 billion
State Street	$29.1 billion
BlackRock	$23.1 billion
Fidelity Investments	$20.2 billion
Capital	$6.4 billion
Morgan Stanley	$5.7 billion
JPMorgan Chase	$4.1 billion
Amundi	$2.3 billion
UBS	$1.9 billion
Allianz/PIMCO	$470 million
Total Titan investments:	$165.7 billion

SABIC (SAUDI ARABIA'S BASIC INDUSTRIES CORPORATION)
2022 REVENUE: $39.8 billion
INSTITUTIONAL OWNERS: Saudi Aramco owns 70 percent

Titan investors in 2022:

Vanguard	$644 million
BlackRock	$437 million
Total Titan investments:	$1.08 billion

BASF, GERMANY
2022 REVENUE: $93 billion
INSTITUTIONAL OWNERS: 367

Titan investors in 2022:

Vanguard	$732 million
Amundi	$538 million
BlackRock	$466 million
Fidelity Investments	$104 million
Total Titan investments:	$1.84 billion

In 2022, the Titans had a total of $192.4 billion invested in the top five plastic manufacturers, making them major contributors to global plastic pollution.

SMALL ARMS AND MASS SHOOTINGS

Gun violence is the leading cause of death for children in the United States. Gun deaths for children and teens rose 50 percent, from 1,731, in 2019, to 2,590, in 2021. In 2021 guns killed more than forty-five thousand Americans. The United States accounts for less than 5 percent of the world's population yet has 46 percent of civilian-owned guns in the world, making it the country with the highest per capita gun ownership. As of 2022 the United States had no federal laws banning semiautomatic assault rifles, handguns, or large-capacity magazines.[1]

In 2021, 690 people in the US were killed in mass shootings; in 2022, 647 were. According to the Gun Violence Archive, mass shooting is defined as an incident in which an attacker

---

1. Jonathan Masters, "U.S. Gun Policy: Global Comparisons," Council on Foreign Relations, last updated June 10, 2022.

kills or wounds four or more people. As of May 2023, there were more than 630 mass shootings in 2023, averaging two mass killings a day for the previous three years.[1]

Although AR-15–style assault rifles have received significant negative news coverage as mass shooters' weapon of choice, handguns are used in most mass shootings.[2] Nonetheless, AR-15–styles and AR-15s have been used in many deadly attacks over the years, including, most recently, in the mass shootings in Uvalde, Texas, and Buffalo, New York, which both occurred in May 2022. Corporate news media typically fails to report the full extent of gun violence and its human and economic costs.[3]

One exception is gun violence in US schools, which, while statistically rare, has been so widely covered in the corporate media that students are experiencing "rising levels of anxiety and other mental-health problems."[4]

Chances of a school shooting in the US remain near .0003 percent; still, since 2020, firearms have been the leading cause of death for children ages one to seventeen—even more likely than motor accidents.[5] Now more than ever, it is impossible to overstate the importance of lawmakers limiting or eliminating access to firearms, especially those with high-capacity magazines, in order to prevent further senseless deaths.[6]

---

1. "How Many US Mass Shootings Have There Been in 2023?," BBC News, May 25, 2023, updated August 27, 2023.

2. Statista Research Department, "Guns Used in Mass Shootings in the U.S. 1982–2023," Statista, August 1, 2023.

3. See, for example, Shealeigh Void, "How Corporate News Distorts Gun Violence," *The Progressive*, July 24, 2023; Lauren Reduzzi and Mickey Huff, "Economic Consequences of US Gun Violence 'Far Costlier' than Previously Known," in *State of the Free Press 2024*, 77–79; and Jonathan Franklin, "How AR-15-Style Rifles Write the Tragic History of America's Mass Shootings," NPR, May 10, 2023.

4. Maya Chung, "School Shootings Are Raising Anxiety and Panic in U.S. Children," *Time*, May 27, 2022.

5. Annette Choi, "Children and Teens Are More Likely to Die by Guns than Anything Else," CNN, March 29, 2023.

6. Sharon Zhang, "2022 Was Worst Year for School Shootings 'by Nearly Every Meaningful Measure,'" Truthout, February 14, 2023.

TITAN INVESTMENTS IN THE
TOP US FIREARM MAKERS

SMITH & WESSON
2022 REVENUE: $864 million
INSTITUTIONAL OWNERS: 366

Titan investors in 2022:

BlackRock	$164 million
Vanguard	$70.1 million
State Street	$32.4 million
UBS	$19.4 million
JPMorgan Chase	$2.2 million
Morgan Stanley	$2.1 million
Fidelity Investments	$423,000
Allianz/PIMCO	$71,000
Total Titan investments:	$290.6 million

STURM, RUGER & COMPANY
2022 REVENUE: $595 million
INSTITUTIONAL OWNERS: 202

Titan investors in 2022:

BlackRock	$183.6 million
Vanguard	$177 million
State Street	$34.9 million
Morgan Stanley	$12.6 million
UBS	$8.7 million
JPMorgan Chase	$3.1 million
Allianz/PIMCO	$659,000
Fidelity Investments	$178,000
Total Titan investments:	$420.7 million

SIG SAUER
2022 REVENUE: $2.78 billion
PRIVATELY OWNED[1]

ANDERSON MANUFACTURING
2022 REVENUE: $44.4 million
PRIVATELY OWNED BY LANCE ANDERSON

GLOCK, AUSTRIA AND GLOCK USA
2022 REVENUE: $66.1 million
PRIVATELY OWNED

Unfortunately, the United States has become the mass-shooting capital of the world and the country with the largest per capita gun ownership. It hardly seems appropriate for supposedly socially sensitive Titan investors to be earning returns from such misery.

GAMBLING COMPANIES AND GAMBLING ADDICTION

The National Council on Problem Gambling estimates the annual social cost of gambling in the United States to be $7 billion, including "gambling-related criminal justice and health-care spending as well as job loss, bankruptcy and other consequences."[2] One percent of gamblers in the United States (approximately two million people) have severe gambling problems, meaning that gambling has negative consequences for them, including financial problems and harmful impacts on relationships and work.[3]

---

1. SIG Sauer is a brand name used by two sister companies based in Germany and the United States. The company, originally based in Germany, was founded in 1976 from a partnership between two other arms companies, Schweizerische Industrie Gesellschaft (SIG) and J. P. Sauer & Sohn.
2. "Health and Treatment: FAQ," National Council on Problem Gambling, accessed August 28, 2023.
3. "Health and Treatment," National Council on Problem Gambling, 2023.

TITAN INVESTORS IN THE LARGEST PUBLICLY TRADED GAMBLING COMPANIES

DRAFTKINGS (SPORTS BETTING), US

2022 REVENUE: $2.24 billion

INSTITUTIONAL OWNERS: 994

Titan investors in 2022:

Vanguard	$1.958 billion
BlackRock	$453 million
Capital	$361 million
State Street	$230 million
UBS	$110.3 million
Allianz/PIMCO	$93 million
Fidelity Investments	$66 million
JPMorgan Chase	$21.1 million
Amundi	$14.8 million
Total Titan investments:	$3.307 billion

CHURCHILL DOWNS INCORPORATED (HORSE RACING), US

2022 REVENUE: $1.8 billion

INSTITUTIONAL OWNERS: 744

Titan investors in 2022:

Vanguard	$1.35 billion
Capital	$990 million
BlackRock	$848 million
Fidelity Investments	$772 million
State Street	$205 million
Morgan Stanley	$49 million
UBS	$20 million
Allianz/PIMCO	$318,340
Total Titan investments:	$4.23 billion

LAS VEGAS SANDS CORPORATION (CASINO GAMBLING)
2022 REVENUE: $4.1 billion
INSTITUTIONAL OWNERS: 1,355

Titan investors in 2022:

Vanguard	$3.66 billion
Capital	$2.1 billion
JPMorgan Chase	$908.9 million
BlackRock	$838 million
State Street	$719 million
Amundi	$183.3 million
Morgan Stanley	$163.6 million
UBS	$148 million
Allianz/PIMCO	$66.9 million
Fidelity Investments	$65.4 million
Total Titan investments:	$8.85 billion

LIGHT & WONDER (GAMING TABLES AND MACHINES)
2022 REVENUE: $2.51 billion

Titan investors in 2022:

Vanguard	$1.247 billion
BlackRock	$895 million
Fidelity Investments	$294 million
Capital	$247 million
State Street	$222 million
Morgan Stanley	$171 million
Total Titan investments:	$3.076 billion

Titans invest $19.193 billion in the four largest gambling companies; a portion of their earnings comes from the more than two million people in the United States who are addicted to gambling.

PRIVATE PRISON COMPANIES

In the US, a number of state governments, as well as the federal government, contract with private corporations to build and manage jails and prisons. The argument for these public-private partnerships is that private businesses can run the facilities more efficiently than governments can. While prison companies may be able to produce greater profits than government-run facilities do, these superior returns are achieved primarily by undercutting salaries and benefits for prison employees and leaving facilities chronically understaffed. In some instances, private prison companies have also actively lobbied to promote state and federal policies that result in more people being incarcerated, a conflict of interest that Project Censored has previously reported on.[1]

A nationwide study found that assaults on guards by inmates were 49 percent more frequent in private prisons than in government-run prisons. The same study revealed that assaults on fellow inmates were 65 percent more frequent in for-profit prisons.[2] Another study concluded that privately operated prisons "appear to have systemic problems in maintaining secure facilities," noting that these prisons have significantly higher rates of homicide, assault, drug abuse, and inmates escaping compared to public facilities.[3] The American Civil Liberties Union (ACLU) reports that US Immigration and Customs

---

1. See, for example, Caitlin Morgan and Peter Phillips, "Private Prison Companies Fund Anti–Immigrant Legislation," in *Censored 2012: Sourcebook for the Media Revolution*, ed. Mickey Huff and Project Censored (New York: Seven Stories Press, 2011), available online at the Project Censored website.
2. James Austin and Garry Coventry, *Emerging Issues on Privatized Prisons* (Washington, DC: Bureau of Justice Assistance, US Department of Justice, February 2021).
3. Brendan Fischer, "Violence, Abuse, and Death at For-Profit Prisons: A GEO Group Rap Sheet," PR Watch, September 26, 2013.

Enforcement (ICE) has expanded its use of private prisons for immigrant control, resulting in widespread grievances documenting the abuse and unnecessary deaths of detainees held in these facilities across the country.[1] Based on independent investigative reports by the *Nation* and *Democracy Now!*, Project Censored has evidenced deadly medical neglect for immigrants held in privatized US jails.[2]

In 2022, the for-profit prison firm GEO Group "made $1.05 billion in revenue from ICE contracts alone, or 43.9 percent of its total revenue ($2.4 billion)," the ACLU reported in August 2023.[3] The ACLU also noted that 30 percent, or $552.2 million, of CoreCivic's 2022 profits derived from ICE detention contracts.[4]

TITAN INVESTORS IN PRIVATE PRISON COMPANIES

GEO GROUP

2022 REVENUE: $2.4 billion

INSTITUTIONAL OWNERS: 437

Titan investors in 2022:

BlackRock	$235.9 million
Vanguard	$109 million
Fidelity Investments	$102.7 million
Vanguard	$86.8 million
State Street	$36.6 million
Morgan Stanley	$6.8 million

---

1. Eunice Hyunhye Cho, "Unchecked Growth: Private Prison Corporations and Immigration Detention, Three Years into the Biden Administration," ACLU News, August 7, 2023.

2. See Aliana Ruiz et al., "Deadly Medical Neglect for Immigrants in Privatized US Jails," in *Censored 2017*, ed. Mickey Huff and Andy Lee Roth with Project Censored (New York: Seven Stories Press, 2016), available online at Project Censored's website.

3. Cho, "Unchecked Growth."

4. Ibid.

Allianz/PIMCO	$2.2 million
JPMorgan Chase	$1.6 million
UBS	$1 million
Total Titan investments:	$582.6 million

CORECIVIC (FORMERLY CORRECTIONS CORPORATION OF AMERICA)
2022 REVENUE: $1.98 billion
INSTITUTIONAL OWNERS: 433

Titan investors in 2022:

BlackRock	$326.2 million
Vanguard	$226.7 million
Fidelity Investments	$210.6 million
State Street	$47.1 million
Allianz/PIMCO	$10.9 million
Morgan Stanley	$9.9 million
JPMorgan Chase	$5.4 million
UBS	$2.5 million
Total Titan investments:	$839.4 million

The two largest publicly traded private prison companies, which both have a history of human rights violations and documented inmate deaths, receive more than $1.42 billion in investment capital from the Titans.

ESG INVESTING AND TITAN HYPOCRISY

Titan companies have all declared a sensitivity to environmental, social, and governance (ESG) investing. They claim that investors seek to influence positive changes in society by using their wealth to promote improved ESG standards. However, the social aspects of ESG investing are mostly ignored by the Titans. Titan investments in tobacco, alcohol, plastics, small arms, gambling, and private prisons raise fundamental questions about their commitment to healthy communities and sustainable environments.

It seems clear that the Titans' ESG investments are based more on profitability than on the social consequences of the goods and services that companies provide. Titan investments support industries that cause grievous harm to the health and well-being of millions of people in the world. If ESG investment standards are to have any meaning, they need to be determined democratically, based on social justice benchmarks rather than financial returns on investments. The Titans will need to learn to accept expert guidance on ESG requirements for their investment practices. The world would be a decidedly better place if the hundreds of billions now invested in socially harmful products and activities were allocated for human betterment.

CHAPTER 5

TITANS' INVESTMENTS IN WAR AND THE INTERNATIONAL WEAPONS TRADE

War and preparation for it are key areas of investment for Titans. In April 2022, the Stockholm International Peace Research Institute (SIPRI) reported that world military spending exceeded US$2 trillion in 2021. That year, military spending was highest in the United States ($801 billion), China ($293 billion), India ($76.6 billion), the UK ($68.4 billion), and Russia ($65.9 billion), according to SIPRI.[1]

One reason for such extreme levels of US military spending is that the country's arms industry is privatized. By contrast, in Russia and China, the primary weapons makers are state-run companies. Privately owned arms manufacturers sell the bulk of their products to the United States and other NATO governments.[2] US-based weapons manufacturers have more institutional shareholders than their European counterparts.

Listed below are the Titans' investments in the top ten Western arms manufacturers for 2022. Defense (war) revenue includes weapon sales to the US Departments of Defense and

---

1. Diego Lopes Da Silva et al., SIPRI (Stockholm International Peace Research Institute), *SIPRI Fact Sheet: Trends in World Military Expenditure*, 2021, April 2022.
2. Ibid.

Homeland Security and US intelligence agencies as well as to international clients.

TITAN INVESTMENTS IN THE TOP TEN WESTERN ARMS MANUFACTURERS

LOCKHEED MARTIN, US
2022 REVENUE: $65.98 billion (96 percent military)[1]
INSTITUTIONAL OWNERS: 3,305

Titan investors in 2022:

Vanguard	$19.72 billion
State Street	$19.033 billion
BlackRock	$7.448 billion
Capital	$7.411 billion
Fidelity Investments	$7.323 billion
Morgan Stanley	$3.78 billion
UBS	$904 million
Total Titan investments:	$65.62 billion

RAYTHEON TECHNOLOGIES, US
2022 REVENUE: $67.07 billion (65 percent military)[2]
INSTITUTIONAL OWNERS: 3,467

Titan investors in 2022:

Vanguard	$19.9 billion
State Street	$14.03 billion
Capital	$13.74 billion
BlackRock	$8.91 billion
Morgan Stanley	$4.94 billion

---

1. Lockheed Martin and its subsidiaries spent $13.6 million on lobbying in 2022. See "Client Profile: Lockheed Martin," OpenSecrets, July 24, 2023.
2. Raytheon Technologies and its subsidiaries spent $10.7 million on lobbying in 2022. See "Client Profile: Raytheon Technologies," OpenSecrets, July 24, 2023.

JPMorgan Chase	$4.36 billion
Fidelity Investments	$1.62 billion
UBS	$482 million
Amundi	$191 million
Allianz/PIMCO	$13.4 million

Total Titan investments:	$68.2 billion

BOEING, US

2022 REVENUE: $66.6 billion[1] (32 percent military in 2023)

INSTITUTIONAL OWNERS: 2,391

Titan investors in 2022:

Vanguard	$16.83 billion
BlackRock	$7.6 billion
State Street	$6.63 billion
Capital	$5.86 billion
Fidelity Investments	$4.67 billion
Morgan Stanley	$1.64 billion
JPMorgan Chase	$851 million
UBS	$580 million
Amundi	$95.1 million
Allianz/PIMCO	$29.3 million

Total Titan investments:	$44.8 billion

---

1. Boeing and its subsidiaries spent $13.1 million on lobbying in 2022. See "Client Profile: Boeing Co," OpenSecrets, July 24, 2023.

GENERAL DYNAMICS, US
2022 REVENUE: $39.4 billion (80 percent military)[1]
INSTITUTIONAL OWNERS: 2,266

Titan investors in 2022:

Vanguard	$8.08 billion
State Street	$2.69 billion
BlackRock	$2.5 billion
JPMorgan Chase	$2.19 billion
Capital	$2.1 billion
Fidelity Investments	$527 million
UBS	$189 million
Allianz/PIMCO	$11.1 million
Amundi	$6.1 million
Total Titan investments:	$18.3 billion

NORTHROP GRUMMAN, US
2022 REVENUE: $36.60 billion (96 percent military)[2]
INSTITUTIONAL OWNERS: 2,363

Titan investors in 2022:

Vanguard	$8.38 billion
State Street	$6.88 billion
Capital	$5.23 billion
BlackRock	$3.04 billion
Fidelity Investments	$2.66 billion
JPMorgan Chase	$1.29 billion
Morgan Stanley	$1.26 billion
UBS	$135 million
Allianz/PIMCO	$26.5 million
Total Titan investments:	$28.9 billion

1. General Dynamics spent $11.5 million on lobbying in 2022. See "Client Profile: General Dynamics," OpenSecrets, July 24, 2023.
2. Northrop Grumman and its subsidiaries spent $10.9 million on lobbying in 2022. See "Client Profile: Northrop Grumman," OpenSecrets, July 24, 2023.

BAE SYSTEMS, UK
2022 REVENUE: $26.29 billion (96 percent military)
INSTITUTIONAL OWNERS: 38

Titan investors in 2022:

Capital	$515 million
BlackRock	$17 million
Vanguard	$11.54 million
Allianz/PIMCO	$2.4 million
Total Titan investments:	$545.9 million

L3HARRIS TECHNOLOGIES, US
2022 REVENUE: $17.06 billion (84 percent military)[1]
INSTITUTIONAL OWNERS: 2,029

Titan investors in 2022:

Vanguard	$5.53 billion
BlackRock	$3.94 billion
Capital	$3.12 billion
State Street	$1.89 billion
Morgan Stanley	$451 million
Fidelity Investments	$414.2 million
UBS	$195 million
JPMorgan Chase	$190 million
Amundi	$58.1 million
Allianz/PIMCO	$4.1 million
Total Titan investments:	$15.8 billion

---

1. L3Harris Technologies and its subsidiaries spent $3.58 million on lobbying in 2022. See "Client Profile: L3Harris Technologies," OpenSecrets, July 24, 2023.

LEONARDO, ITALY

2022 REVENUE: $15.45 billion (83 percent military)

INSTITUTIONAL OWNERS: 157 (the Italian government holds a 30 percent share)

Titan investors in 2022:

Vanguard	$101.5 million
Fidelity Investments	$22.9 million
State Street	$1.06 million
JPMorgan Chase	$744,000
Allianz/PIMCO	$158,000
BlackRock	$23,000
Total Titan investments:	$126.39 million

THALES GROUP, FRANCE

2022 REVENUE: $19.18 billion (53 percent military)

INSTITUTIONAL OWNERS: 378 (the French government owns more
than 26 percent; Dassault Aviation holds nearly 25 percent)

Titan investors in 2022:

Vanguard	$395 million
Capital	$263.7 million
State Street	$14.2 million
JPMorgan Chase	$12.43 million
BlackRock	$286,000
Allianz/PIMCO	$38,000
Fidelity Investments	$23,000
Total Titan investments:	$685.7 million

LEIDOS, US

2022 REVENUE: $14.4 billion (58 percent military)[1]
INSTITUTIONAL OWNERS: 1,267

Titan investors in 2022:

Vanguard	$1.28 billion
BlackRock	$609 million
State Street	$463.3 million
JPMorgan Chase	$360.3 million
Total Titan investments:	$2.7 billion

In aggregate, Titan investments in the top ten Western military contractors for 2022 amounted to more than $265.6 billion.

As indicated, the companies that produce weapons for the United States and NATO are highly dependent on capital investments from the Titans and many thousands of smaller capital investment companies. To ensure their share of the United States' lucrative annual budget for military spending, the defense industry spent $126.5 million on lobbying in 2022, according to OpenSecrets.[2] The watchdog site also noted that more than 72 percent of the lobbyists representing the defense industry are former government officials.

BlackRock maintains an iShares US Aerospace & Defense exchange-traded fund for investors. Launched in May 2006, the fund now has net assets of $5.782 billion. It's been evaluated by Morgan Stanley Capital International (MSCI), which describes itself as the "leading provider of critical decision support tools and services for the global investment community." MSCI noted

---

1. Leidos was formerly known as Science Applications International Corporation. Leidos and its subsidiaries spent $2.83 million on lobbying in 2022. See "Client Profile: Leidos Inc," OpenSecrets, July 24, 2023.
2. "Sector Profile: Defense," OpenSecrets, July 24, 2023.

that the BlackRock Aerospace & Defense fund does not use a sustainability, impact, or ESG investment strategy: 34 percent of the businesses involved have controversial weapons such as cluster munitions, landmines, depleted uranium weapons, biological and chemical weapons, blinding lasers, nondetectable fragments, and incendiary weapons, and 24.27 percent of the businesses are involved with manufacturing nuclear weapons, including nuclear warheads, intercontinental ballistic missiles, and ballistic missile submarines.[1]

BlackRock describes the performance of the Aerospace & Defense fund by charting the growth of a $10,000 investment made on May 1, 2006. A $10,000 investment then would be worth $59,776 in June 2023, offering a 597 percent increase over the seventeen-year period.

All of the US weapons makers listed above are included in BlackRock's portfolio. Wealth concentration seems to work really well when investing in military weapons contractors.

The United States has been in a state of permanent war since World War II. These wars and military actions contribute greatly to the profitability of the defense industry in the US in which Titans are deeply invested.

AMERICAN WARS SINCE THE END OF WORLD WAR II

INVASIONS

Korean War (1950–1953), Vietnam War (1955–1975), Cuba: Bay of Pigs (1961), Lebanon (1982–1984), Grenada (1983), Libya bombing (1984), Persian Gulf: Tanker War (1984–1987), Panama (1989–

---

1. "iShares U.S. Aerospace & Defense ETF," iShares (BlackRock), 2023.

1990), Gulf War (1989–1991), Iraq War (1991–1993), Bosnian War (1992–1995), Haiti (1994–1999), Kosovo (1998–1999), Afghanistan (2001–2021), Yemen (2002–present), Iraq War (2003–2011), Pakistan (2004–2018), Somalia (2007–present), Libya (2011), Niger (2013–present), Iraq (2014–2021), Syria (2014–present), Libya (2015–2019), Ukraine (2021–present)

CIVIL WARS

Indochina (1959–1975), Indonesia (1958–1961), Lebanon (1958), Dominican Republic (1965), Korea DMZ (1966–1969), Cambodia (1967–1975), Somalia (1991–present)[1]

Permanent war spending is a critical economic stimulus for corporate capitalism. Weapons manufacturers and their investors are, in a sense, addicted to military conflict and spending in preparation for it. For example, stock shares of military and security firms surged when Russia invaded Ukraine in February 2022.[2] Some weeks into the conflict, shares of Raytheon stock rose by 8 percent, General Dynamics by 12 percent, Lockheed Martin by 18 percent, and Northrop Grumman by 22 percent, while war stocks in Europe, India, and elsewhere experienced similar surges in expectation of an exponential rise in global military spending.[3]

Global superpowers reached the height of military insanity

1. Joseph H. Chung, "America's Perpetual War: Six Questions," Global Research, July 15, 2023; see also Deepa Kumar, "Play It Again, (Uncle) Sam: A Brief History of US Imperialism, Propaganda, and News," in *Censored 2015: Inspiring We the People*, eds. Andy Lee Roth and Mickey Huff with Project Censored (New York: Seven Stories Press, 2014), 295–314.

2. See, for example, Robin Andersen, "Guns, Guns, Guns: Criminal Justice, Mass Shootings, and War: News Abuse in 2021–2022," in *State of the Free Press 2024*, especially 189–93.

3. Edward Helmore, "Defense and Cybersecurity Stocks Climb amid Russia's Invasion of Ukraine," *The Guardian*, February 28, 2022; Asit Manohar, "Russia-Ukraine War: Defence Spending to Surge. Experts Bullish on These Stocks," Mint, March 2, 2022; and William I. Robinson, "Global Capitalism Has Become Dependent on War-Making to Sustain Itself," Truthout, April 24, 2022.

during the Cold War, developing thousands of nuclear weapons and their global delivery systems. Expanded arsenals were declared necessary as a deterrence so each of the belligerents knew they would be destroyed in a nuclear exchange. Even though Russia and the United States have agreed to stop building new nuclear weapons—knowing that what each nation already possesses is more than enough to destroy life on Earth—both countries continue to replace and upgrade their existing nuclear arsenals. The Congressional Budget Office estimates that "plans for US nuclear forces, as described in the fiscal year 2021 budget and supporting documents, would cost $634 billion over the 2021–2030 period," for an average of more than $60 billion per year.[1]

LARGEST NATIONAL NUCLEAR ARSENALS, BY NUMBER OF WARHEADS (2023)[2]

1.	Russia	4,489
2.	United States	3,708
3.	China	410
4.	France	290
5.	United Kingdom	225
6.	Pakistan	170
7.	India	164
8.	Israel	90
9.	North Korea	30
	WORLD TOTAL	9,576

The Treaty on the Prohibition of Nuclear Weapons, "a comprehensive set of prohibitions on participating in any nuclear

1. "Projected Costs of U.S. Nuclear Forces, 2021 to 2030," Congressional Budget Office, May 24, 2021.
2. Max Roser, Bastian Herre, and Joe Hasell, "Nuclear Weapons: Stockpiles of Nuclear Weapons," Our World in Data, Oxford Martin School, University of Oxford, accessed August 31, 2023.

weapon activities," opened for signature on September 20, 2017, and entered into force on January 22, 2021.[1] The treaty, which has ninety-two national signatories to date, prohibits all aspects of developing, possessing, or threatening to use nuclear weapons. However, none of the nine nuclear-armed nations— Russia, the United States, China, France, the United Kingdom, Pakistan, India, Israel, and North Korea—recognizes the treaty.[2] Instead, these nine countries wasted $82.9 billion on nuclear weapons production and maintenance in 2022, according to a report from the International Campaign to Abolish Nuclear Weapons (ICAN).[3] This amount of money could eliminate world hunger by feeding one billion people annually.[4]

I believe the only way to ensure that nuclear weapons will never be used again is for the United States to unilaterally destroy all its nuclear weapons. The United States built the first atomic bombs and is the only nation to have used nuclear weapons in combat. For that reason, numerous Catholic bishops, Pope Francis, and many others believe that possession of nuclear weapons is immoral.[5] The United States has a moral obligation to take the first step toward the total elimination of all nuclear weapons and to invite the eight additional nuclear-armed nations to do the same. The argument that US nuclear weapons are necessary as a deterrent is false. If China or Russia were to bomb the United States, that act would be a death warrant for them and everyone else in the world; the resulting

---

1. "Treaty on the Prohibition of Nuclear Weapons," United Nations, Office for Disarmament Affairs, accessed September 1, 2023.
2. Jon Letman, "The US Has No Plans to Give Up Nuclear Weapons. The Public Needs to Change That," Truthout, April 24, 2023.
3. *Wasted: 2022 Global Nuclear Weapons Spending* (International Campaign to Abolish Nuclear Weapons, June 2023).
4. "How Much Would It Cost to End World Hunger?," World Food Program USA, August 10, 2022.
5. "Pope on Hiroshima: Possession of Nuclear Weapons 'Immoral,'" *Washington Post*, August 6, 2020.

nuclear winter would slowly kill all human life on Earth. We must acknowledge that spending billions on nuclear weapons only benefits the atomic arms industry and its Titan-led investors. It is in the self-interest of the weapons makers to lobby their governments for the continuation of high levels of military spending on nuclear weapons, using deterrence as a false rationale.

President Dwight D. Eisenhower's 1953 observation remains timely: "Every gun that is made, every warship launched, every rocket fired signifies, in the final sense, a theft from those who hunger and are not fed, those who are cold and are not clothed."[1]

NUCLEAR WEAPONS PRODUCERS AND TITAN SHAREHOLDERS, LOAN PROVIDERS, AND BOND HOLDERS

The Titans are heavily invested in companies that profit from nuclear weapons production. The data in the following list of nuclear weapons producers is sourced from ICAN's 2021 report, *Perilous Profiteering*.[2]

AEROJET ROCKETDYNE (SUBSIDIARY OF L3HARRIS), US
NUCLEAR WEAPONS REVENUE (2022): $4 million

Builds solid boost propulsion systems used with land- and sea-based nuclear ballistic missile systems.

---

1. Dwight D. Eisenhower, "'The Chance for Peace' Address Delivered before the American Society of Newspaper Editors, April 16th, 1953," Dwight D. Eisenhower Presidential Library (National Archives), accessed August 28, 2023.

2. Susi Snyder, "Perilous Profiteering: The Companies Building Nuclear Arsenals and Their Financial Backers," PAX and ICAN (International Campaign to Abolish Nuclear Weapons), November 2021.

Titan investors: BlackRock, Fidelity Investments, JPMorgan Chase, Morgan Stanley, State Street, Vanguard

Total Titan investments in 2022: $2.31 billion

AIRBUS GROUP, NETHERLANDS
NUCLEAR WEAPONS REVENUE (2022): unreported

Builds ballistic missiles used by France in partnership with BAE Systems.

Titan investor: Vanguard, $718 million

LEONARDO, ITALY
NUCLEAR WEAPONS REVENUE (2022): unreported

Involved in the design, development, and delivery of transporter erector replacement vehicles for the US Minuteman III intercontinental ballistic missile (ICBM) fleet. Also involved in the production of medium-range air-to-surface nuclear missiles for France.

Titan investors: BlackRock, Capital Group, Amundi, Fidelity Investments, JPMorgan Chase, Morgan Stanley, UBS, Vanguard

Total Titan investments in 2022: $126.39 million

BAE SYSTEMS, UK
NUCLEAR WEAPONS REVENUE (2022): $844 million

Supports arsenals of the UK, France, and US; Minuteman III ICBM, UK Trident II D5.

Titan Investors: BlackRock, Capital Group, Amundi, JPMorgan Chase, Morgan Stanley, State Street, Vanguard

Total Titan investments in 2022: $545.9 million

BECHTEL GROUP, US
NUCLEAR WEAPONS REVENUE (2022): $1.6 billion

Operates Lawrence Livermore National Laboratory, nuclear weapons research, and improved ICBM technologies.

Privately held by Bechtel family.

BOEING, US
NUCLEAR WEAPONS REVENUE (2022): $892 million

Production of Minuteman III and Trident II D5 missiles, B61-12 nuclear gravity bombs, air-launched cruise missiles.

Titan investors: BlackRock, Capital Group, Amundi, Fidelity Investments, JPMorgan Chase, Morgan Stanley, State Street, UBS, Vanguard

Total Titan investments in 2022: $44.8 billion

GENERAL DYNAMICS, US
NUCLEAR WEAPONS REVENUE (2022): $2.7 billion

Produces nuclear submarines that feature Trident II D5 ballistic missiles.

Titan investors: BlackRock, Capital Group, Fidelity Investments, JPMorgan Chase, State Street, Vanguard

Total Titan investments in 2022: $18.3 billion

HONEYWELL INTERNATIONAL, US
NUCLEAR WEAPONS REVENUE (2022): $6.5 billion

Produces key components for nuclear weapons; manages several US nuclear weapons production facilities, including Sandia National Laboratories; produces guidance systems for Minuteman III ICBM.

Titan investors: Amundi, JPMorgan Chase, Morgan Stanley, Vanguard

Total Titan investments in 2022: $38.9 billion

HUNTINGTON INGALLS INDUSTRIES, US
NUCLEAR WEAPONS REVENUE (2022): $847 million

Provides personnel and equipment for pit production at Los Alamos National Laboratory.

Titan investors: Allianz/PIMCO, BlackRock, Capital Group, Fidelity Investments, JPMorgan Chase, Morgan Stanley, State Street, Vanguard

Total Titan investments in 2022: $4.02 billion

LEIDOS, US
NUCLEAR WEAPONS REVENUE (2022): $3.3 billion

Part of one of the largest US federal contractors, Consolidated Nuclear Security, which manages Pantex, the primary US nuclear weapons assembly plant, and the Y-12 National Security Complex.

Titan investors: BlackRock, JPMorgan Chase, State Street, Vanguard

Total Titan investments in 2022: $2.7 billion

LOCKHEED MARTIN, US
NUCLEAR WEAPONS REVENUE (2022): $2 billion

Designed reentry systems for Minuteman III ICBM, constructed Trident II D5 missiles for UK and US, engineering for Trident II Fleet Ballistic Missile System.

Titan investors: BlackRock, Capital Group, Amundi, JPMorgan Chase, Morgan Stanley, State Street, UBS, Vanguard

Total Titan investments in 2022: $65.62 billion

NORTHROP GRUMMAN, US
NUCLEAR WEAPONS REVENUE (2022): $9.6 billion

Designed fixed wings for the B61-12 nuclear gravity bomb and propulsion systems for Trident II D5 missiles.

Titan investors: BlackRock, Capital Group, Fidelity

Investments, JPMorgan Chase, Morgan Stanley, State Street, Vanguard

Total Titan investments in 2022: $28.9 billion

ARIANEGROUP, FRANCE
NUCLEAR WEAPONS REVENUE (2022): unreported

Maintenance of French M51 submarine-launched ballistic missiles, development of M51 modifications.

Titan investors: BlackRock, Vanguard, Capital Group, Amundi, Fidelity Investments

Total Titan investments in 2022: $222 million

TITAN MILITARISM EQUALS
MORAL BANKRUPTCY

When it comes to investment returns from war-making, the Titans are global leaders, with more than $265.6 billion invested in the world's top ten weapons-producing companies. From tanks to nuclear weapons, the Titans are deeply embedded in the US and NATO global military empire. Real wars improve these corporations' bottom lines and yield extravagant dividends to investors. Continuing threats from alleged terrorists, communists, and noncooperating governments are justifications for national governments' continued investments in conventional and nuclear weapons. War spending is also one of the primary mechanisms for increasing the concentration of capital among the top .05 percent and consequently the continuation of mass inequality and hunger around the world.

Titan investments in the Western global war economy are built on the unending threat of war. Actual wars and the continuous readiness for war push the world arms investment returns toward an inevitable extinction-level event that will be accidental or deliberately provoked. The insanity of militarism as promoted by Titan capital investments seeking to maximize returns from military contractors is nothing less than a morally bankrupt circumstance that threatens human civilization on our planet.

CHAPTER 6

CHINA

Building a Multipolar World

In 1978, China opened its economy to reforms that allowed private capital growth and economic expansion. China's gross domestic product has grown by an average of 9 percent annually since then. During that time, some eight hundred million people were lifted out of extreme poverty (a term that applies to those living on $2.15 a day or less), allowing China to report, in 2021, significant improvements in health, education, and human services nationwide and the complete elimination of extreme poverty. However, it is estimated that six hundred million people in China still earn about $150 a month.[1]

China now has a burgeoning middle class, with millions of families who own homes and cars and have personal holdings. In 2021, 350 million households (1.01 billion people) earned 160,000 yuan ($22,359) or higher.[2] Life expectancy in China is now 78.1 years and exceeds the US life expectancy of 76.1 years.[3] China has identified a standard for human rights where

---

1. Alexander Smith and Robbie Hu, "China Created More Billionaires than the U.S. Now It Is Cracking Down," NBC News, September 5, 2021.

2. Daniel Zipser et al., *2023 McKinsey China Consumer Report: A Time of Resilience* (McKinsey & Company, December 2022).

3. Mary Hui, "China's Life Expectancy Is Now Higher than That of the US," Quartz, September 1, 2022.

the goal is a "moderately prosperous society," or *Xiaokang* society, in which all people are neither rich nor poor but free from want and toil—in other words, they are basically well-off.[1] Geopolitical analyst Mike Whitney writes, "A World Bank report recently highlighted the huge drop in global poverty rates from 1980 to 2008, but critics noted that over 100 percent of that decline came from China alone: the number of Chinese living in dire poverty fell by a remarkable 662 million, while the impoverished population in the rest of the world actually rose by 13 million."[2]

China, officially the People's Republic of China (PRC), is ruled by the Chinese Communist Party (CCP), founded in 1921. After winning a civil war, the CCP took military control of mainland China in 1949. The losing Kuomintang government found refuge on the island of Taiwan, which remains separate from China and is a continuing source of political tension.

China's State Council is composed of the premier and the heads of each governmental department and agency, under the guidance of the CCP. The current CCP general secretary, Xi Jinping, is now in his third five-year term, having been reapproved by the ninety-million-member CCP in 2022. Although China is officially communist, in 2014, *China Daily*, an English-language daily newspaper produced by the Central Propaganda Department of the CCP, reported that "China will allow all forms of capital to equally compete in the financial market through ease of market access," according to then Chinese premier Li Keqiang.[3] In 2023 *Forbes* reported that the

1. Kim Peterson, "China Eliminated Absolute Poverty; Now Works toward Common Prosperity for All," Countercurrents.org, February 1, 2023.
2. Mike Whitney, "China's Turn. America's Hyper-Financialized Economic System Is No Match for China's Government-Directed Investment Model," Global Research, March 3, 2023.
3. "China Vows Equal Financial Market Competition for All Capital," *China Today*, September 27, 2014.

United States was home to 735 billionaires; China (including Hong Kong and Macau) was second, with 562 billionaires.[1]

China initiated its Belt and Road Initiative in 2013. Since then the country has provided more than $5 trillion to 147 nations for infrastructure improvements, including ports, rail lines, energy projects, and roadways that offer opportunities for improving trade agreements between China and other countries. The broader agenda of the Belt and Road Initiative is to promote China's centralized state planning as a model for economic development and to build global links for increased trade.[2]

China is rapidly reaching an economic base on par with the United States. Depending on the source, China has already surpassed the United States in economic terms or will do so within a few years. In 2014, the International Monetary Fund identified China as the world's largest economy.[3]

Its assessment considered not only GDP but also purchasing power parity (PPP) as measures of economic power.[4] The United States has continued to claim that China's GDP is only at 80 percent of the US GDP and that China will not surpass the United States for several more years. Either way, it is likely that, even after a steep setback in 2021 due to the global pandemic, China's accelerated growth rate will likely pass that of the United States in the near future.[5] In July 2023 economist Richard D. Wolff wrote:

---

1. Rob LaFranco and Chase Peterson-Withorn, eds., "World's Billionaires List: The Richest in 2024," *Forbes*, accessed September 21, 2023.

2. *A World Divided: Russia, China and the West* (Bennett Institute for Public Policy, University of Cambridge, October 20, 2022).

3. See, for example, Mike Bird, "China Just Overtook the US as the World's Largest Economy," Business Insider, October 8, 2014.

4. On purchasing power parity, see Tim Callen, "PPP versus the Market: Which Weight Matters?," *Finance & Development* 44, no. 1 (March 2007). *Finance & Development* is published by the IMF.

5. "Comparing United States and China by Economy," Statistics Times, May 15, 2021.

China's economy gained more (especially in GDP growth) from neoliberal globalization than Western Europe, North America, and Japan did. China grew fast enough to compete now with capitalism's old centers. The decline of the U.S. within a changing world economy has contributed to the crisis of U.S. capitalism. For the U.S. empire that arose out of World War II, China and its BRICS allies represent its first serious, sustained economic challenge. The official U.S. reaction to these changes so far has been a mix of resentment, provocation, and denial. Those are neither solutions to the crisis nor successful adjustments to a changed reality.[1]

Many in the United States are concerned that it will lose global status as the top economy in the world, causing the value of the US dollar to decline. Certainly a recalibration of economic power is in progress. Argentina has recently allowed banks to open deposits to the Chinese yuan due to an acute shortage of dollar reserves. Argentina's central bank indicated that "the measure is complementary to the decision of the National Securities Commission (CNV), which enabled the negotiation of negotiable securities in yuan" for local financial markets, teleSUR reported in June 2023.[2]

The United States remains the top country for trade with Latin America, but China hit a new export high of $265 billion to Latin America in 2022, with a corresponding $184 billion of Latin American imports that year. China and Ecuador established a free trade agreement in 2023. El Salvador canceled its fifteen-year-old trade agreement with Taiwan in favor of its trade with China. Brazil and

1. Richard D. Wolff, "Why Capitalism Is Leaving the U.S., in Search of Profit," Countercurrents. org, July 20, 2023.
2. "Argentina Enables Deposits in Yuan for Local Bank Accounts," teleSUR English, June 30, 2023.

China have agreed to conduct trade using the Chinese yuan and are cooperating to manufacture satellites. Nicaragua and China have initiated import and export tariff cuts.[1]

Threats posed by China to the United States have been widely discussed in US corporate media and fanned by the US State Department and other agencies, including the CIA. Numerous news stories regarding China engaging in aggressive actions in the South China Sea, using "spy balloons" over US territory, and establishing clandestine listening posts in Cuba have been reported frequently. Corporate media has also covered continuing military near-misses in the air or at sea, framing them as evidence of rising tensions between the two nations in anticipation of US House Speaker Nancy Pelosi's August 2022 visit to Taiwan. The Pentagon has not apologized to China for shooting down the runaway weather balloon and falsely reporting it was a spying device. Pentagon spokesman Brigadier General Pat Ryder acknowledged, "It has been our assessment now that [the spy balloon] did not collect [data] while it was transiting the United States."[2] The existence of a Chinese listening station in Cuba is a matter of pure speculation.

Taiwan has remained separated from mainland China since 1949. It is not politically recognized as an independent nation by most countries in the world, including the US. But it maintains an independent economy, government, and military. China officially claims Taiwan is legally its territory, but the Chinese have not attempted a military invasion. The Titans hold investments in a number of corporations in Taiwan, including the largest company in Taiwan, TSMC, a semiconductor manufacturing firm.

1. Ralph Jennings, "5 Trade Moves China Has Made in 2023 in Latin America—the Traditional Backyard of the US," *South China Morning Post*, May 20, 2023.
2. Chloe Kim, "Chinese Spy Balloon Did Not Collect Information, Says Pentagon," BBC News, June 29, 2023.

TAIWAN SEMICONDUCTOR MANUFACTURING
COMPANY LIMITED (TSMC)
2022 REVENUE: $73.67 billion

INSTITUTIONAL OWNERS: 2,187

Titan investors in 2022:

JPMorgan Chase	$5.374 billion
Fidelity Investments	$2.473 billion
Morgan Stanley	$2.292 billion
Vanguard	$2.266 billion
BlackRock	$1.168 billion
UBS	$602.5 million
State Street	$336 million
Amundi	$237 million
Allianz/PIMCO	$50 million
Total Titan investments	$14.8 billion

In a serious threat to China, in July 2023, the United States authorized $345 million in military support to Taiwan, including Reaper drones (produced by General Atomics), Harpoon antiship missiles (McDonnell Douglas), Stinger antiaircraft missiles (Raytheon), and TOW antitank missiles (Raytheon). This support is part of a billion-dollar military aid package the United States is providing to Taiwan. The weapons provided are from existing US stocks, but they are likely to be replaced by new orders, earning more profits for arms manufacturers and Titan investors.[1]

American public opinion toward China has changed dramatically over the past five years. In 2018 less than half of all Americans held negative opinions toward China. In 2023 that number now exceeds 80 percent.[2]

---

1. Gary Wilson, "Biden Sends $345 Million in Weapons to Taiwan: Activists Protest U.S.-Australia Anti-China War Games," Struggle La Lucha, August 2, 2023.
2. Ian Prasad Philbrick, "If Biden Wanted to Ease U.S.-China Tensions, Would Americans Let Him?," *New York Times*, June 27, 2023.

China continues to violate civil liberties, as reported by Human Rights Watch. In Xinjiang, the organization reported:

> Despite government propaganda portraying its policies in the region as successful efforts to counter terrorism, international scrutiny of crimes against humanity in the region grew. In May [2022], an anonymous source released hacked police files from the region, which included nearly 3,000 photos of Uyghur detainees, along with key policy documents outlining harsh policies from China's top leadership. As many as a million people were wrongfully detained in political education camps, pretrial detention centers, and prisons at the height of the Strike Hard Campaign.[1]

In Tibet, authorities continue to enforce "severe restrictions on freedoms of religion, expression, movement, and assembly. Popular concerns over issues such as mass relocation, environmental degradation, or the phasing out of the Tibetan language in primary education were met with repression."[2] And, in Hong Kong, "national security police raided the office of influential media outlet Stand News on December 29, 2021, charged its editors with sedition, and effectively forced it to close; this prompted seven other outlets to close within two weeks. In April, police arrested the ex-Stand News columnist and veteran journalist Allen [sic] Au on baseless charges of sedition."[3]

In the 2020 report *The Elements of the China Challenge*, the US State Department characterized China as a challenge "because of its conduct" and noted that the Chinese Com-

---

1. Tirana Hassan, "World Report: China, Events of 2022," Human Rights Watch, 2023.
2. Ibid.
3. Hassan, "China, Events of 2022."

munist Party is "modeled on 20th-century Marxist-Leninist dictatorship."[1] Despite significant economic growth based on China's decision to embrace free market elements, the State Department argued that the CCP uses "its economic power to co-opt and coerce countries around the world" and to "reshape international organizations in line with China's brand of socialism." By seeking "national rejuvenation," the report asserted, China aimed at complete "transformation of the international order."

That China has had remarkable economic growth is undisputed. Despite some elements of corruption being reported inside the government, socioeconomic human betterment in China is noteworthy. As reported by the World Trade Organization in 2023, China's exports of goods in 2021 totaled $3.363 trillion, and imports came to $2.688 trillion.[2] Overall, in 2020, China boasted the largest share of global trade at 11.5 percent, surpassing the US trade share of 11.1 percent.[3] Between 2007 and 2017, China more than doubled the size of its highway system, from thirty-four thousand miles of roads to more than eighty-one thousand. China also heavily developed its subway and now has eight of the world's twelve longest subway systems.[4]

A 2020 executive order issued by President Trump restricted US individuals and firms from investing in publicly traded securities from firms that the US Treasury designated as Chinese Military Companies. The executive order was intended

1. *The Elements of the China Challenge* (US Office of the Secretary of State, November 2020, updated December 2020).

2. "Chinese Foreign Trade in Figures," Santander Trade Portal, Analyze Market Trends, Santander, last updated July 2023.

3. Xie Jun and Liu Yang, "WTO Entry a Milestone for China: Yiwu Traders," *Global Times*, December 7, 2021.

4. Yuen Yuen Ang, "The Robber Barons of Beijing: Can China Survive Its Gilded Age?," *Foreign Affairs*, June 22, 2021.

to ensure that no US investments supported China's military modernization.[1]

Private capital investment in China is widespread and growing annually. China's opening of its economy to private investments has paved the way for building a strong middle-class country. The Titans have responded accordingly.

Titans are strongly invested in the top twelve firms in China. These investments are only a portion of the $1.3 trillion invested in China through Wall Street stock exchanges; however, the Titans are leaders in capital investing in China's burgeoning economy.

TITAN INVESTMENT IN KEY CHINESE FIRMS

TENCENT HOLDINGS
2022 REVENUE: $823.5 billion

Internet services, mobile applications, online gaming platforms, instant messaging systems, gaming software, photo downloading software, online payment systems.

INSTITUTIONAL OWNERS: 88

Titan investors in 2022:

Vanguard	$9.013 billion
JPMorgan Chase	$1.216 billion
Fidelity Investments	$46.5 million
BlackRock	$40.3 million
Total Titan investments:	$10.3 billion

---

1. Martin Chorzempa, "New Rules Curbing Us Investment in China Will Be Tricky to Implement," Peterson Institute for International Economics, May 3, 2023.

CHINA STATE CONSTRUCTION ENGINEERING CORPORATION
2022 REVENUE: $524.8 billion

Housing construction engineering, real estate development and investment, international engineering.

INSTITUTIONAL OWNERS: 25 (the state-owned assets supervision and administration commission of the State Council holds a 57.1 percent share)

Titan investors in 2022:

Vanguard	$63.2 million
Fidelity Investments	$36.5 million
BlackRock	$21.5 million
Allianz/PIMCO	$20.1 million
Morgan Stanley	$15.16 million
Total Titan investments	$156.4 million

SINOPEC
2022 REVENUE: $482.6 billion

Exploration, development, and production of crude oil and natural gas.

INSTITUTIONAL OWNERS: 75 (the Chinese government owns 94 percent of the company)

Titan investors in 2022:

Vanguard	$121 million
BlackRock	$59.5 million
Fidelity Investments	$35.2 million
Allianz/PIMCO	$1.14 million
State Street	$819,000
Total Titan investments:	$217.2 million

PETROCHINA COMPANY
2022 REVENUE: $479.13 billion

Oil company with a network of more than eighteen thousand
filling stations.

INSTITUTIONAL OWNERS: 76

Titan investors in 2022:

Allianz/PIMCO	$75.58 million
BlackRock	$64.5 million
Vanguard	$55.9 million
Fidelity Investments	$4.58 million
State Street	$4.29 million
JPMorgan Chase	$303,000
Total Titan investments:	$205.2 million

STATE GRID CORPORATION OF CHINA
2022 REVENUE: $461 billion

World's largest electric utility.

INSTITUTIONAL OWNERS: state-owned assets supervision
and administration commission, 61.8 percent; government
of China, 7.9 percent

Titan investors in 2022:

Vanguard	$9 million

INDUSTRIAL AND COMMERCIAL BANK OF CHINA
2022 REVENUE: $209 billion

INSTITUTIONAL OWNERS: 261

Titan investors in 2022:

Vanguard	$1.7 billion
BlackRock	$216.5 million
Fidelity Investments	$119.7 million
JPMorgan Chase	$42.5 million
Morgan Stanley	$21.7 million
State Street	$18.3 million
Allianz/PIMCO	$2.16 million

Total Titan investments:	$2.12 billion

CHINA LIFE ASSET MANAGEMENT COMPANY
(SUBSIDIARY OF CHINA LIFE INSURANCE COMPANY)
2022 REVENUE: $167 billion

INSTITUTIONAL OWNERS: 153

Titan investors in 2022:

Vanguard	$442.7 million
Fidelity Investments	$427 million
BlackRock	$234.3 million
State Street	$26 million
JPMorgan Chase	$8.7 million
Allianz/PIMCO	$483,000

Total Titan investments:	$1.14 billion

AGRICULTURAL BANK OF CHINA
2022 REVENUE: $102.78 billion
INSTITUTIONAL OWNERS: 192

Titan investors in 2022:

Vanguard	$363.5 million
BlackRock	$234 million
Fidelity Investments	$89 million
State Street	$20.8 million
JPMorgan Chase	$795,000
Allianz/PIMCO	$249,000

Total Titan investments:	$708.3 million

CHINA CONSTRUCTION BANK
2022 REVENUE: $115.4 billion
INSTITUTIONAL OWNERS: 296

Titan investors in 2022:

Vanguard	$2.3 billion
Fidelity Investments	$374 million
BlackRock	$135.7 million
State Street	$105.4 million
Allianz/PIMCO	$56.1 million
JPMorgan Chase	$14.6 million

Total Titan investments:	$2.98 billion

CHINA UNITED NETWORK COMMUNICATIONS GROUP (CHINA UNICOM)
2022 REVENUE: $48.2 billion
INSTITUTIONAL OWNERS: 762

Titan investors in 2022:

Vanguard	$45.1 million
BlackRock	$40.57 million
Fidelity Investments	$7.32 million
Allianz/PIMCO	$617,000
JPMorgan Chase	$560,000
State Street	$502,000
Total Titan investments:	$94.6 million

ALIBABA GROUP HOLDING LIMITED
2022 REVENUE: $35.92 billion

Multinational specializing in e-commerce, retail, and technology.

INSTITUTIONAL OWNERS: 922

Titan investors in 2022:

Vanguard	$1.82 billion
Fidelity Investments	$735 million
BlackRock	$670.5 million
JPMorgan Chase	$488 million
UBS	$246 million
Amundi	$112.6 million
Allianz/PIMCO	$33.9 million
Total Titan investments:	$4.11 billion

BAIDU
2022 REVENUE: $17.9 billion

Technology multinational specializing in internet-related services, cloud computing, and artificial intelligence.

INSTITUTIONAL OWNERS: 777

Titan investors in 2022:

BlackRock	$2.18 billion
Vanguard	$1.29 billion
Morgan Stanley	$516.8 million
UBS	$157.8 million
Fidelity Investments	$80.4 million
JPMorgan Chase	$78.2 million
State Street	$37 million
Amundi	$28.3 million
Allianz/PIMCO	$5.8 million
Total Titan investments:	$4.37 billion

Titans held $29.5 billion of investments in the leading twelve companies in China in 2022. All ten Titan companies have active investment offices in China, providing opportunities for Westerners to invest directly in Chinese companies and for Chinese citizens to invest in Western markets.

China has the longest and most-used high-speed rail system in the world. The PRC began construction on it in 2007, and it now connects all of mainland China. The network represents two-thirds of the world's total mileage of high-speed railways. China plans to expand the system to forty-three thousand miles by 2035.

CHINA STATE RAILWAY GROUP COMPANY
2022 REVENUE: $168.24 billion

Titan investors in 2022:

Vanguard	$99.8 million
BlackRock	$39.9 million
Fidelity Investments	$19.5 million
Allianz/PIMCO	$922,000
State Street	$869,000
Total Titan investments:	$160.99 million

China has a growing capital asset management industry. Their top thirty asset management companies manage a combined $5.9 trillion in wealth. The largest company is the China Life Asset Management Company (cited above), with $217.7 billion in assets under management in 2021. Six Titan-directed asset management companies held $1.14 billion in China Life shares in 2022. While the top thirty Chinese investment management firms still only control around 10 percent of what the top ten Western Titan firms manage, they continue to increase wealth concentration at a rate equal to or higher than their Western counterparts. Chinese-owned asset management companies are attractive investments for Titan capital.

CHINA AND THE WORLD ECONOMIC FORUM

Xi Jinping, president of the People's Republic of China, was invited to give keynote speeches at the World Economic Forum in Davos in 2017 and 2022. In 2017 Xi addressed the inadequacy of globalization to meet the pressing needs of the world's poor by identifying three root causes, including "lack of robust driving forces for global growth," "inadequate global economic governance," and "uneven global development."[1] Xi continued:

> The richest 1 percent of the world's population own more wealth than the remaining 99 percent. Inequality in income distribution and uneven development space are worrying. Over 700 million people in the world are still living in extreme poverty. For many families, to have warm houses, enough food, and secure jobs is still a distant dream. This is the biggest challenge facing the world today.

In his 2022 address to the World Economic Forum, Xi emphasized the need for global cooperation in the aftermath of the COVID-19 pandemic. He called for efforts to bridge the "development divide" and to revitalize global development:

> The process of global development is suffering from severe disruption, entailing more outstanding problems like a widening North-South gap, divergent recovery trajectories, development fault lines, and a technological divide. . . . The world's poor population has increased by more than one hundred million. Nearly eight hundred million people live in hunger.[2]

Addressing those challenges, Xi contended, requires discarding a "Cold War mentality" and seeking "peaceful coexistence and win-win outcomes." Noting that China would remain com-

---

1. "Full Text of Xi Jinping Keynote at the World Economic Forum," CGTN America (China Global Television Network), January 17, 2017.
2. "Full Text: Address by Xi at 2022 World Economic Forum Virtual Session," *China Daily*, January 17, 2022.

mitted to "promoting ecological conservation," Xi identified carbon neutrality as an "intrinsic" requirement of China's development.

Xi's vision is deeply grounded in the concept noted earlier in this chapter—Xiaokang, creating a moderately prosperous society. His position is that the Chinese Communist Party is promoting Xiaokang—or modest levels of work, health, and betterment—for all humans in the world.

There is compatibility between Xi's vision of Xiaokang and the WEF's concept of "stakeholder capitalism" and its ESG framework. China is taking an active role in WEF events by sending full delegations to Davos and hosting the WEF's Annual Meeting of the New Champions, held in Tianjin in June 2023.

China's premier, Li Qiang, gave the welcoming remarks to the 1,500 attendees at the New Champions meeting, calling for a post-COVID reopening of globalization and free trade, with open communication, cooperation, and world peace.[1]

WORLD ECONOMIC FORUM ATTENDEES AT DAVOS FROM THE PEOPLE'S REPUBLIC OF CHINA, 2023

China is playing an increasingly active role in the WEF, as is evident from the following list of public officials and corporate leaders who attended the Davos meetings in 2023:

---

1. "AMNC23: Premier Li Qiang's Opening Remarks at the 14th Annual Meeting of the New Champions," World Economic Forum, June 29, 2023.

PUBLIC OFFICIALS

Liu He	Chinese vice premier, WEF keynote speaker 2023
Wang Shouwen	China international trade rep and vice minister of commerce
Yi Gang	Former governor, People's Bank of China
Fang Xinghai	Vice chair, China Securities Regulatory Commission
Liao Min	Vice minister of finance, People's Republic of China
Weng Jieming	Vice chair, State-owned Assets Supervision and Administration Commission

CORPORATE LEADERS

Zhao Ying	President, Ant Group
Hu Shuli	Publisher, Caixin Media
Li Xin	Managing director, Caixin Media
Mei Yan	Managing director, China Global Television Network
Tian Wei	Host: *World Insight*, China Global Television Network
Lei Zhang	CEO, Envision Group
Cherie Nursalim	Vice chair, Giti Group
Scott Beaumont	President, Google Asia Pacific
Claire Cromier Thielke	China-Head, Hines Asia Pacific
Yang Yuanqing	CEO, Lenovo
Raymund Chao	Chair-CEO, PwC
Theo Bertram	VP, public policy, TikTok
Ralf Brandstätter	China management, Volkswagen
Liming Chen	Chair, Greater China, World Economic Forum
Lin Boqiang	Dean, Energy Policy, Xiamen University
Miranda Qu Fang	Founder, Xiaohongshu
Christy Lei Sun	Chief of marketing, Yatsen Global
Gong Yingying	CEO/founder, Yidu Tech

China's increasingly deep involvement with the WEF indicates its willingness to accept a multipolar world economy that addresses human betterment for a global society. China's promotion of Xiaokang, as well as its WEF-affiliated corporations lining up in support of stakeholder capitalism and ESG values, are shared steps on an aligned path.

However, both Chinese and Western firms continue to emit increasing amounts of global-warming gases and to profit from alcohol, tobacco, and plastics. Chinese capital can be just as exploitative as Western capital toward workers, abroad and internally. The Chinese Communist Party tolerates little in the way of worker democracy and labor union activity, which remains firmly under state control.[1] Chinese billionaires are accepted as builders of the capital necessary for economic growth, but unlike in the United States, where money openly buys political influence, billionaires in China must still kowtow to the party.

The Titans who hold a core share of global investment capital retain shares in both Chinese and Western companies. As a result, the Titans need to be taking a larger role in addressing global cooperation and steering the United States and NATO away from aggression against China and into a more productive direction of planned multipolar engagement instead.

---

1. William I. Robinson, "The Unbearable Manicheanism of the 'Anti-Imperialist' Left," The Philosophical Salon, August 7, 2023.

CHAPTER 7

RUSSIA

An Ideological Challenge to Global Capitalism

The Russian government under Vladimir Putin has inherited the remnants of the former Soviet Union (USSR), including a vast arsenal of nuclear weapons. Once the foremost communist country, the Russian Federation today is a shell of its former self. Putin has been Russia's prime minister or president since 1999.

At the end of World War II, the USSR occupied several nations in Eastern Europe, supporting (or imposing) the establishment of communist governments. Fearful of further Soviet incursions into Europe and ideologically challenged by communism, Western European countries, along with the US and Canada, joined together in an alliance of mutual self-defense. The North Atlantic Treaty Organization was founded in 1949 as a twelve-nation security agreement for this purpose.[1]

The United States and its NATO allies engaged in a cold war with the Soviet Union, finally achieving the latter's negotiated dismantling in 1991. After 1991 Russia experienced severe economic depression, losing 50 percent of its gross domestic product and suffering hyperinflation of over 200 percent annually, from 1991 to 1994. The poverty rate ($5.50 a day) soared to over 50 percent.

---

1. "Founding Treaty," NATO (North Atlantic Treaty Organization), September 2, 2022.

Part of the negotiations among the USSR and the US and other NATO nations was a promise that NATO would not expand its boundaries to include nations that were formerly territories of the Soviet Union. The late Russia-studies expert Stephen F. Cohen noted this history in a piece for the *Nation* in 2018. Cohen wrote, "Washington broke its promise not to expand NATO 'one inch eastward.'" [1] In early 1990 then president George H. W. Bush's secretary of state, James Baker, acted as a major conduit for communicating this message to Russian leaders at the time, but he was not alone. Cohen went on, writing, "All of the Western powers involved—the US, the UK, France, Germany itself—made the same promise to Gorbachev on multiple occasions and in various emphatic ways. At that time, Baker concurred with Gorbachev: "NATO expansion is unacceptable."[2]

However, Russia was still seen as a military and economic threat by the US and NATO. Nations that were formerly territories of the Soviet Union—including Estonia, Bulgaria, Czechia, Hungary, Latvia, Lithuania, Poland, Romania, and Slovakia—joined NATO when invited. It should be noted that NATO armed forces have always been under the command of US generals or admirals.[3]

Bush recognized the other independent republics emerging from the USSR and established diplomatic relations with Russia, Ukraine, Belarus, Kazakhstan, Armenia, and Kyrgyzstan. In February 1992 Baker visited the remaining republics, and diplomatic relations were established with Uzbekistan,

---

1. Stephen F. Cohen, "The US 'Betrayed' Russia, but It Is Not 'News That's Fit to Print,'" *The Nation*, January 10, 2018; see also Edward B. Winslow, "The US/NATO Gambit in Ukraine: A Proxy War for World Hegemony," Global Research, June 28, 2022.
2. Ibid.
3. Ibid.

Moldova, Azerbaijan, Turkmenistan, and Tajikistan. Civil war in Georgia prevented its recognition and the establishment of diplomatic relations with the US until May 1992.[1] The 1990 GDP of the USSR was $2.66 trillion, a little less than half of the US GDP of $5.9 trillion. The old Soviet economy had been based on state ownership of the means of production and state control of investments. By 2022, under a semiprivatized model of capitalism, Russia's GDP had fallen to $2.4 trillion. Meanwhile, US GDP had risen to $25.4 trillion.[2]

The United States and NATO had long hoped to weaken Russia further by encouraging Ukraine to join NATO. In 2014 the US supported a regime change in Ukraine as anti-Russian civilians engaged in unrest, known as the Maidan Revolution, leading to the removal of democratically elected Ukrainian president Viktor Yanukovych. An anti-Russian government quickly emerged, with some neo-Nazi elements in support. Yanukovych was forced to flee to Russia. To protect its Black Sea navy and warm-water ports, Russia responded by using military forces to occupy Crimea, declaring it was no longer part of Ukraine. Russia justified its annexation by pointing out that ethnic Russians constitute 80 percent of Crimea's population. US president Barack Obama initiated sanctions against the Russian Federation on December 14, 2014, prohibiting the export of goods and services to the region.

Donetsk and Luhansk, with large, majority-Russian ethnicities, had faced attacks by Ukraine after 2014 when the Donetsk People's Republic and the Luhansk People's Republic

1. "The Collapse of the Soviet Union," Office of the Historian, Foreign Service Institute, United States Department of State, accessed August 25, 2023.
2. "United States," World Bank, accessed August 25, 2023; and "GDP (Current US$)—Russian-Federation," World Bank, accessed August 25, 2023.

declared independence from Ukraine. Russia provided military support to the new republics, claiming that they were justified in seeking independence after years of incessant shelling by Ukrainian forces.[1] Russia declared their military forces were on a "peacekeeping mission" to protect ethnic Russians in the Donbas region in eastern Ukraine.[2] Seeking to prevent Ukraine from joining NATO and striving to protect Russian ethnicities in the region, military forces of the Russian Federation launched a limited "special military operation" that crossed Ukraine's borders on February 24, 2022, in support of provincial forces of Donetsk and Luhansk seeking independence from Ukraine. Russia also directly attacked Ukraine's capital, Kyiv.

US corporate media described the Russian support of the new republics as an unprovoked invasion and widely condemned Russia's military advances in the region. For example, on February 24, 2022, *PBS NewsHour* described the Russian actions as "a full-scale invasion . . . that could rewrite the global post-Cold War security order."[3] Just two days earlier, on February 22, 2022, the US Treasury had imposed expanded sanctions on the top Russian banks in response to Putin's recognition of Donetsk and Luhansk as independent states.

The Russian Federation is still geographically the world's largest nation and home to massive amounts of natural resources, including vast oil and gas reserves. Russian resources are highly coveted by global investment capital. When given the opportunity, the Titans have invested widely in Russian enterprises. However, the US Treasury restricted capital investment in the Russian Federation after Russia engaged directly

1. Winslow, "The US/NATO Gambit."
2. Ibid.
3. Yuras Karmanau et al., "Russia Invades Ukraine on Multiple Fronts in 'Brutal Act of War,'" *PBS NewsHour*, February 24, 2022.

in an ongoing civil war in Ukraine. The Treasury gave US capital investment companies until May 25, 2022, to freeze their holdings in five Russian companies, including VTB Bank, the second-largest bank in Russia, and the Russian investment company VEB. At the time, BlackRock's Emerging Markets exchange-traded fund (ETF), worth an estimated $16 billion, included debt issued by VEB, while a second BlackRock ETF, "designed to give investors exposure to Russian stocks, had a stake of almost $2 million in VTB," the *Los Angeles Times* reported.[1]

On March 7, 2022, Reuters reported that Vanguard and BlackRock would suspend all purchases of Russian securities. The Moscow Stock Exchange has been closed for most trading since February 28, 2022, and the London Stock Exchange, Nasdaq, and New York Stock Exchange have since suspended trading in most Russian companies.[2] Vanguard reported that its remaining funds would adhere to all sanction rules for Russia, noting that its Russian securities amounted to less than 0.01 percent of its clients' assets. If accurate, Vanguard's exposure in Russia amounts to $8 billion.[3] BlackRock acknowledged a loss of $17 billion after Russia engaged militarily in Ukraine. BlackRock also claimed that the loss represented less than 0.01 percent of its total funds.[4]

A January 2023 article published by *Politico* reported that most Western companies are doing business as usual in Russia,

1. Silla Brush and Loukia Gyftopoulou, "How Will American Financial Institutions Deal with Russia Sanctions?," *Los Angeles Times*, February 25, 2022.
2. David Hayes, "Top Investors in Russia's Sberbank, VTB Bank Face Billions in Losses," S&P Global, March 10, 2022.
3. "Russian Sanctions, Index Changes, and Vanguard Funds," Vanguard, March 3, 2022, last updated March 9, 2022.
4. James Phillipps, "BlackRock Funds Suffer $17BN Losses on Russia Exposure," Citywire, March 14, 2022.

despite the ongoing war.[1] Only about 8 percent of European Union firms have divested from Russia, with the largest number of still-active firms based in Germany. Around 18 percent of US firms accounted for the highest level of exits.[2] While McDonald's had left Russia, Subway remained active, *Politico* reported. A Yale University study of companies that had left Russia by July 2023 found 32 percent were from the US, 10.6 percent from the UK, 7.8 percent from Germany, and less than 5 percent from all other countries.[3]

TITAN INVESTMENTS IN RUSSIAN COMPANIES

VTB BANK

2022 REVENUE: $21.3 billion

INSTITUTIONAL OWNERS: The Russian government's Federal Agency for State Property Management holds nearly 61 percent of the shares.

Note: VTB closed its investment bank in London in response to western sanctions.

Titan frozen shares in 2022:

Titan	Number of Shares	Estimated Value of Losses
Vanguard	135.9 billion	$25 million
BlackRock	24.7 billion	$10.5 million
JPMorgan Chase	168 million	$2.8 million
State Street	891 million	$1.6 million
Fidelity Investments	102.8 billion	unreported

---

1. Wilhelmine Preussen and Nicholas Camut, "Majority of Western Companies Doing Business as Usual in Russia, Study Finds," *Politico*, January 19, 2023.

2. See, for example, Lawrence White, "Russia's VTB Closes London-Based Investment Bank as Sanctions Bite," Reuters, March 15, 2022.

3. Jeffrey Sonnenfeld and Yale Research Team, "Yale CELI List of Companies Leaving and Staying in Russia," Chief Executive Leadership Institute, Yale School of Management, last updated August 29, 2023.

Allianz/PIMCO	92.7 million	unreported
Amundi	24.46 billion	unreported

SBERBANK, VEB.RF

2021 REVENUE: $39.2 billion

INSTITUTIONAL OWNERS: VEB is a legal nonprofit corporation

Titan frozen shares in 2022:

Titan	Number of Shares	Estimated Value of Losses
Capital	> 200 million	$537.1 million
Vanguard	303.9 million	$314 million
JPMorgan Chase	> 6.3 million	$191.7 million
Amundi	5.033 million	$148 million
Fidelity Investments	84.28 million	$128 million
UBS	3.568 million	$105 million
BlackRock	181.25 million	$103.5 million
Allianz/PIMCO	696,762	$20.9 million

GAZPROM

2020 REVENUE: $87.7 billion

Even before Gazprom's ability to export gas to Europe was seriously curtailed following the September 2022 explosions that disabled two of its Nord Stream gas pipelines, the company had sought to expand its gas distribution to involve client nations to the east, including China.[1]

INSTITUTIONAL OWNERSHIP: The Russian government
controls 50 percent of shares

---

1. "Pressure Drops in Nord Stream Pipelines as Gas Leaks into Sea," bne IntelliNews, September 27, 2022; James Henderson, "Comment: Can Russia Pivot Its European Gas Sales to Asia?," bne IntelliNews, August 12, 2022.

Titan investors from 2021 who sold their shares include Vanguard, JPMorgan Chase, State Street, Allianz/PIMCO, and Capital Group.

Titan investors remaining in 2022:

BlackRock	3.6 million shares	value unknown
Fidelity Investments	828,000 shares	value unknown
JPMorgan Chase	43,000 shares	value unknown

ROSNEFT

2022 REVENUE: $93.5 billion

As Russia invaded Ukraine, BP promised to sell its nearly 20 percent stake in Russia's largest oil company, Rosneft. In December 2022 Global Witness reported that BP had been unable to sell its shares and that, consequently, BP continued to receive dividends from Rosneft, which were worth an estimated £580 million (approximately $706 million at then-current exchange rates).[1] However, BP's "wartime windfall" was to be held in a restricted Russian bank account that could only be accessed for withdrawals with Russian government approval. BP would write off its full investment, according to the Global Witness report.

In most cases, the Titans lost equity value in their stock holdings in Russia, which were minor compared to their full holdings. The losses were offset by an increase in the values of investments, worth $265.6 billion, that the Titans held in military weapons manufacturers. Shares in Lockheed Martin, Raytheon, Boeing, Northrop Grumman, and General Dynamics appreciated in value nearly 13 percent on average in the one-year span after the Russian invasion of Ukraine. These

---

1. "What BP Could Do with Its £580M Wartime Russian Oil Profits," Global Witness, December 2, 2022.

increases represent approximately $30 billion in financial gains for the Titans.[1]

Due to the war with Ukraine, Russia discontinued its involvement in the World Economic Forum. Historically, Russia's Roscongress Foundation would host Russia House at the WEF's annual meetings in Davos, with many international delegates paying visits. However, after Russia's conflict with Ukraine began, the WEF declared Russia unwelcome in Davos. The former Russia House premises now host the Ukraine delegation.

The separation from Davos encouraged Russia to place greater emphasis on its St. Petersburg International Economic Forum, which has been held each June for twenty-seven years. SPIEF 2023 hosted seventeen thousand people from 130 countries. The Russian News Agency TASS reported that important national leaders attending in 2023 included Armenian president Vahagn Khachaturyan, South Ossetian president Alan Gagloyev, Cuban prime minister Manuel Marrero Cruz, and the chairman of Kyrgyzstan's Cabinet of Ministers, Akylbek Japarov. The United Arab Emirates participated in the forum as an official guest nation.[2]

Russia also hosted the second Russia–Africa Summit, July 27 to 28, in St. Petersburg, under the slogan "For peace, security and development."[3] Summit participants called for "increasing cooperation at the highest level and promoting constructive dialogue within the framework of existing international, regional, multilateral and bilateral Russian-African mechanisms on a wide range of strategic, political and economic issues of mutual interest," teleSUR reported.

---

1. Eli Clifton, "Ukraine War Is Great for the Portfolio, as Defense Stocks Enjoy a Banner Year," *Responsible Statecraft*, February 24, 2023.
2. "High-Ranking Officials from over 15 Countries to Attend SPIEF 2023, Kremlin Aide Says," *TASS*, June 14, 2023.
3. "Russia-Africa Summit Ends with Signing of Final Declaration," *teleSUR English*, July 28, 2023.

Economist Richard D. Wolff explains why the sanctions on Russia are somewhat ineffective:

> The Ukraine war has exposed key effects of capitalism's geographic movements and the accelerated economic decline of the U.S. relative to the economic rise of China. Thus the U.S.-led sanctions war against Russia failed to crush the ruble or collapse the Russian economy. That failure has followed in good part because Russia obtained crucial support from the alliances (BRICS) already built around China. Those alliances, enriched by both foreign and domestic capitalists' investments, especially in China and India, provided alternative markets when sanctions closed off Western markets to Russian exports.[1]

NATO's expansion toward the Russian Federation undoubtedly challenged Russia and the US-coordinated actions against the pro-Russian government in Kyiv in 2014 and further threatened Russia's security. Some argue that US interests should use the Russian invasion to further undermine Russia. For example, Raj Verma and Björn Alexander Düben wrote:

> The Russian invasion of Ukraine presents an opportunity for the United States to cement and reaffirm its preeminent position in the international arena. The conflict is expected to significantly undermine Russian military and economic capabilities in the coming years, reducing its role as a great power. This is due, in part, to the ongoing provision of sophisticated weapon sys-

---

1. Wolff, "Why Capitalism Is Leaving the U.S."

tems to Ukraine by Washington and its allies, as well as a comprehensive range of sanctions readily imposed against Moscow.[1]

The long-range goal of Western interests and the Titans is the eventual opening of Russia to unregulated capital investment— new opportunities that will promote continued capital growth and ensure capitalism's growth into the middle of the twenty-first century. That outcome is not guaranteed, however, and this is why NATO's posture toward Russia has become even more aggressive, including threats of an expanded war in the region.

In July 2023 NATO held a summit in the Lithuanian capital, Vilnius. Attendees included heads of state, delegates from Finland (NATO's newest member) and prospective member Sweden, and Ukrainian president Volodymyr Zelensky. Nonmember states attending included Australia, Japan, New Zealand, the Republic of Korea, Georgia, Moldova, and Bosnia and Herzegovina, as well as the president of the European Council. The summit issued a communiqué addressing the war in Ukraine and threats by Russia and China as the justification for a new "NATO-Ukraine Council":

> The Russian Federation is the most significant and direct threat to Allies' security and to peace and stability in the Euro-Atlantic area. Terrorism, in all its forms and manifestations, is the most direct asymmetric threat to the security of our citizens and to international peace and prosperity. . . . The People's Republic of China's (PRC) stated ambitions and coercive policies challenge

1. Raj Verma and Björn Alexander Düben, "Russia's Invasion of Ukraine: Cementing US Global Preeminence," *Journal of Indo-Pacific Affairs* 6, no. 3 (March–April 2023): 74–91.

our interests, security and values. . . . Russia bears full responsibility for its illegal, unjustifiable, and unprovoked war of aggression against Ukraine. . . . We do not and will never recognize Russia's illegal and illegitimate annexations, including Crimea. . . . We have decided to establish the NATO-Ukraine Council, a new joint body where Allies and Ukraine sit as equal members to advance political dialogue, engagement, cooperation, and Ukraine's Euro-Atlantic aspirations for membership in NATO. . . . [Members of NATO] reaffirmed our decisions at the Madrid Summit to put in place additional robust in-place combat-ready forces on NATO's Eastern Flank, to be scaled up from the existing battlegroups to brigade-size units where and when required, underpinned by credible rapidly available reinforcements, prepositioned equipment, and enhanced command and control.[1]

The bulletin essentially presented a hard-line challenge to Russia that the war in Ukraine is not negotiable in nature and, if left unresolved, will result in Russia facing a complete military response from the United States and its NATO allies. It seems that the US–NATO agenda is still to weaken Russia in the hopes of toppling Putin's government and opening Russia to widespread capital investment. The US and NATO seek the reversal of the Putin regime to the period immediately after the USSR dismantling, when Western capital was free to openly invest in Russia under then president Boris Yeltsin. Opening up widespread capital investment in Russia could temporarily

---

1. "Vilnius Summit Communiqué," NATO (North Atlantic Treaty Organization), July 11, 2023, last updated July 19, 2023.

solve the Titans' problem of surplus capital by offering investment opportunities throughout the greater Russian landmass.
However, the obvious risk of this strategy is that it could eco-
nomically backfire, leading to massive capital losses and to a
more recalcitrant Russia, armed and ready for a full nuclear
exchange.

CHAPTER 8

CRASH OF THE TITANS
Building a Better World

WHAT NEEDS TO BE DONE?

In the preface, I posed three sociological questions: To what extent do the wealthy influence—or even dominate—decision-making that affects all members of society? Who are the most powerful people? And how do these processes of influence or domination work?

We can now conclude that the 117 people on the boards of directors of the ten largest capital investment management companies in the world are indeed the Titans of global capitalism. Their decision-making power over $50 trillion of investment capital makes them dominant in the global market. They represent what the White House described in the October 2022 *National Security Strategy* report as "America's vital interests."[1] While the White House described American values as rooted in democracy, the Titans manifest democracy as the unlimited freedom to concentrate capital wealth for .05 percent of the world's population, thereby making these forty million rich people even wealthier.

---

1. The White House, National Security Strategy (Washington, DC: The White House, October 2022).

In addition, the Titans sit on the boards of directors of 133 corporations, for which the collective total annual revenue was more than $4.54 trillion in 2022. These 133 companies—networked to each other through the Titans' boards—have a combined annual revenue greater than the GDP for each of the individual nations in the world except the United States, China, and Japan.[1]

The Titans are the financial core of concentrated global capital; the US government and allied "democratic" governments continue to serve their interests.

Society is pervasively impacted by the Titans' investment choices. As analyzed in Chapter 4, alcohol, tobacco, and gambling addictions are profitable investments for the Titans. Millions of addicted people feed their daily cravings by spending money on behaviors known to be unhealthy and habit-forming. Addicted people's needs are deepened by the creation of a physical dependency often so severe that it can lead to illegal acts to acquire the money needed to satisfy cravings.

Titans are also heavily invested in plastics, which are littering the world's oceans; meanwhile, there is little to no evidence of efforts to remediate the pollution. According to the United Nations Environment Programme, "Exposure to plastics can harm human health, potentially affecting fertility, hormonal, metabolic and neurological activity."[2]

Firearms producers are heavily supported by Titan investment funds. The United States has less than 5 percent of the world's population but is home to 46 percent of the world's civilian-owned guns, making it the country with the highest per capita gun ownership on Earth. Some 71,600 licensed gun

1. "Top 15 Countries by GDP in 2022," Global PEO Services, accessed August 25, 2023.
2. "Campaign to Beat Plastic Pollution," UN Environment Programme.

dealers in the United States sold 16.5 million guns to the public in 2022.[1] That year, there were still no federal laws in America banning semiautomatic assault rifles, handguns, or large-capacity ammunition magazines.[2]

The Titans also continue to invest in private prison companies, thus perpetuating a taxpayer-subsidized, private-profit industry that produces wealth for investors at the cost of inmate deaths and compromised human rights and health, not to mention security issues.

One of the most dangerous Titan investments is the money they provide to companies releasing carbon dioxide and other global warming gases. Titan investments of $432.2 billion permit fossil fuel companies to continue to release global warming gases to the point that human life is threatened and may already be permanently endangered. The summer of 2023 was the warmest on record and likely the hottest in 120,000 years.[3] One would think the Titans would realize their investments in oil, gas, coal, and natural gas are funding expanded releases of global warming gases that threaten all human life, including their own and those of their family members. Perhaps they believe the ESG investment propaganda claiming that fossil fuel companies are sensitive to the environment and that there are decades left to remedy the situation. Perhaps investors believe the ESG claims of their asset management companies; i.e., that all we need are reasonable long-term adjustments, investments in renewable energy sources (such as solar and wind), and new carbon dioxide removal technologies. Perhaps they believe that addressing the real impacts of the climate crisis through carbon offset programs,

---

1. Chip Brownlee, "Gun Violence in 2022, by the Numbers," *The Trace*, December 30, 2022.
2. Masters, "U.S. Gun Policy."
3. Andrea Thompson, "July 2023 Is Hottest Month Ever Recorded on Earth," *Scientific American*, July 27, 2023.

which dramatically overstate actual reductions in carbon emissions, will protect all of us.[1]

The global-warming companies have known for decades that their products are directly related to the transformation of the world's climate.[2] Given their vast information networks, the Titans should have recognized their complicity in our emerging environmental disaster. It is time for the Titans and their ilk to acknowledge their responsibility in allowing a worldwide environmental crisis to develop that foreshadows the deterioration of the quality of human life and all living things on our planet.

The most immediately dangerous of Titan investments are their holdings in the top ten military weapons manufacturers, which amounted to $265.6 billion in 2022. These companies are building the weapons and systems for conventional and nuclear war that could quickly destroy the planet. The Bulletin of the Atomic Scientists' doomsday clock is the closest it has ever been to midnight, highlighting the imminent threats posed by war in Ukraine and the potential for a full confrontation between NATO and Russia. However, as analyzed in Chapters 5 and 7, long-term war in Ukraine and the possibility of regime change in Russia offer the Titans and their clients the prospect of immensely profitable investment opportunities to come. Expanded military spending by the United States and other NATO nations enriches the military companies and their Titan investors while opening up significant postwar investment opportunities for the Titans.

The World Bank estimates that Ukraine will need $411 bil-

---

1. Koruga and Huff, "Certified Rainforest Carbon Offsets Mostly 'Worthless.'"
2. See, for example, Clare Charlesworth and Rob Williams, "Shell Understood Climate Change as Early as 1991—and Ignored It," in *Censored 2018: Press Freedoms in a "Post-Truth" World*, eds. Andy Lee Roth and Mickey Huff with Project Censored (New York: Seven Stories Press, 2017), 77–79. Accessible online in Project Censored's archive of its annual Top 25 story lists.

lion to rebuild after the war. The UK and Ukraine hosted the Ukraine Recovery Conference in June 2023 to mobilize international support for Ukraine's economic recovery during and after the war.[1] The Ukraine Recovery Conference actually predates the Russian invasion in 2022, having begun in 2017. BlackRock and other Titans were actively planning investments in Ukraine even before the Russian invasion in February 2022. Larry Fink, CEO of BlackRock, held a video conference call with Ukraine president Volodymyr Zelensky in September 2022. The call included confirmation of a previous agreement that BlackRock would be the primary adviser to Ukraine in its effort to ensure the foreign investment required for the nation's full recovery after the war. In November 2022 a memorandum of understanding was signed by the BlackRock Financial Markets Advisory Group and the Ukrainian Ministry of Economy, stating that BlackRock would develop a plan for investment in reconstruction funding.[2] The plans included Zelensky attending the World Economic Forum as an invited speaker in Davos, in January 2023, and support for Ukraine using the vacant Russia House to host participants.[3]

The mobilization of global investment capital for Ukraine is a direct challenge to Russia. As of summer 2023, the US and other NATO countries have supplied Ukraine with vast amounts of military equipment including tanks, munitions, and air defense capabilities valued at more than $100 billion. In addition to weapons, the Titans and other Western capitalists are investing in Ukraine's economy. In early 2023, for example,

1. "Ukraine Recovery Conference," 2023.
2. Andrew Moran, "Zelenskyy, BlackRock Announce New Investment Initiative to Rebuild Ukraine," The Epoch Times, December 28, 2022, updated January 11, 2023.
3. Hannah Nightingale, "Zelensky Announces He Is Planning to Join World Economic Forum in Davos, to Sign New Postwar Loans with BlackRock," The Post Millennial, December 28, 2022.

Nestlé announced a $43 million project to construct a new production facility in Western Ukraine. International Finance Corporation, the private investment arm of the World Bank, launched a $2 billion aid package to support Ukraine's private sector. Tattarang, an Australian private investment group, provided $500 million for a Ukraine Green Growth Initiative.[1]

By supporting a pro-Western regime change in Ukraine in 2014, US and NATO intelligence agencies set up the Russian Federation to respond militarily in Ukraine because the US and NATO understood that Russia would never relinquish its warm-water naval ports in Crimea. Russia is now involved in a seemingly unwinnable war that will continue to cost Russian lives and drain Russian resources. The cost in Ukrainian lives is proportionally greater, as Ukraine is one-fifth the size of Russia. The danger is that the war could go nuclear if Russia feels seriously threatened as a nation-state and if the Putin regime remains in power. In the hopes of seeing Putin replaced, the United States, NATO, and the Titans of Capital are playing a dangerous game of chicken with the highest of stakes. That said, prolonged but conventional military conflict offers higher profits to the Titans through increased military spending and postwar-rebuilding investment opportunities.

Titan investments in China are widespread. As analyzed in Chapter 6, Western capital investment in China exceeds $1.3 trillion, with the Titans holding a major share. Challenged ideologically by the Chinese Communist Party and the clear evidence that China's economic power is matching its own, the United States has increasingly turned to propaganda to magnify perceived Chinese threats and minimize its actual successes. Foremost among those perceived threats is China's

---

1. Moran, "Zelenskyy, BlackRock Announce."

increased military budget, including expanded naval forces and hypersonic nuclear weapons. But China's defense was only a third of the US defense budget in 2021.[1]

The likelihood of Taiwan gaining independence from China has also been a point of contention and a possible trigger for military conflict between the US and China, even though the US officially recognizes China's political rights to the island. In August 2023, the White House authorized the Department of the Treasury, in consultation with the Department of Commerce, to develop a new regulatory system for US investments in Chinese security technologies or products, including advanced semiconductors, supercomputers, and quantum computing technologies.[2] The Titans will undoubtedly have to be more careful in their investments in China, but the restrictions are primarily limited to the military sector of the Chinese economy. Any new restrictions implemented by the treasury and commerce departments may be crafted in part to protect the Titan investments of more than $14.8 billion in Taiwan's TSMC, which is the world's most valuable semiconductor manufacturer.

Alleged Chinese threats to the United States and Taiwan are used to justify maintaining US military spending at record levels and the refurbishing of nuclear weapons at Los Alamos National Laboratory, in New Mexico.[3] The restrictions on investments in advanced semiconductors, supercomputers, and quantum computing may also be linked to the Department of

---

1. In 2021, China's defense budget was estimated to be $293 billion, and the US defense budget was an estimated $801 billion. See "World Military Expenditure Passes $2 Trillion for First Time," Stockholm International Peace Research Institute (SIPRI), April 25, 2022.

2. Sarah Bauerle Danzman and Emily Weinstein, "A New White House Order Is Taking Aim at Investment in Chinese Tech. How Will It Actually Work?," New Atlanticist (Atlantic Council), August 10, 2023.

3. Lora Lucero, "Arms Race = Suicide Race," Progressive Democrats of America, Central New Mexico, June 27, 2023.

Defense's (DOD) desire to implement a global 5G sonar and laser network to track and operate missiles and unmanned vehicles "across all domains," including land, sea, air, and space.[1] At the heart of the DOD's Joint All-Domain Command and Control system is the development of a data storage cloud to help track and coordinate the systems of each branch of the US military. In December 2022 the DOD awarded contracts to Amazon, Google, Microsoft, and Oracle for a combined total of up to $9 billion to begin the research required to develop a military cloud computing system.[2]

The Titans are heavily invested in each of the Big Tech companies contracted by the DOD to develop its Joint Warfighting Cloud Capability. Titan investors in Amazon include Vanguard ($169 billion), BlackRock ($59 billion), State Street ($55 billion), Fidelity Investments ($46 billion), Capital ($12 billion), and JPMorgan Chase ($12 billion). Titan investors in Google (Alphabet Inc.) include Vanguard ($88 billion), BlackRock ($33.5 billion), State Street ($30 billion), Fidelity Investments ($11.5 billion), Capital ($10 billion), and JPMorgan Chase ($6.4 billion). The Titans are also invested in Microsoft—including Vanguard ($386 billion) and BlackRock ($138 billion)—and Oracle, in which State Street holds $127 billion, Fidelity Investments $87 billion, and Capital $82 billion.

In combination, Titan investments in the technology companies that will lead the development of the Pentagon's global-war management system exceed $1.4 trillion.

---

1. Department of Defense, *Summary of the Joint All-Domain Command & Control* (JADC2) Strategy, March 2022. On the potential environmental impacts of the joint military and industry efforts to develop the JADC2 system, see Jensen Giesick and Amber Yang, "'Smart Ocean' Technology Endangers Whales and Intensifies Climate Change," in *State of the Free Press 2023*, 71–73. Accessible online in Project Censored's archive of its annual Top 25 story lists.

2. See, for example, Brian Fung, "Pentagon Awards Multibillion-Dollar Cloud Contract to Amazon, Google, Microsoft and Oracle," CNN Business, December 8, 2022.

While the United States seeks to develop its fully functional Joint All-Domain Command and Control system, Russia has inaugurated its own National Defense Management Center to assess global threats and initiate military actions when deemed necessary. And, for its part, China is reported to be developing its Multi-Domain Precision Warfare capabilities, using artificial intelligence and computer networks to rapidly identify key vulnerabilities in the US military system.[1]

It seems evident that Russia and China would be primary targets of the United States' own Joint All-Domain Command and Control system. It also seems that the prime financial beneficiaries of this system will be the Titans and the forty million millionaires and billionaires whose wealth around the world they manage and multiply. The Titans of Capital contribute to the creation of people so rich that democratically elected politicians—if we still have them—would be so beholden to wealth that any independent political thought would be almost completely co-opted by procapitalist propaganda and capital-controlled media and education systems.[2]

It is imperative to ask how we can reverse the concentration of Titan wealth and recertify a grassroots democracy not controlled by wealth. There is no easy answer to this question.

Andrew Ahern writes on the idea of "degrowth" as the equitable downscaling of aggregate production and consumption, especially aimed at the world's highest-consuming (rich) nations and the globally wealthy. The goal of degrowth is to bring the

---

1. Michael T. Klare, "AI vs AI: Flash War and Human Extinction," CounterPunch, July 13, 2023.
2. This possibility is not speculative. For the impacts of "dark money" on US political processes and democracy, see, for example, Kira Levenson and Allison Butler, "Dark Money Interference in US Politics Undermines Democracy," and Zach McNanna and Steve Macek, "New Laws Preventing Dark Money Disclosures Sweep the Nation," both in Project Censored's *State of the Free Press 2024*. Both the "Dark Money Interference" and "New Laws Preventing" stories are accessible online through the Project Censored website.

economy back into balance with the Earth and to thereby achieve well-being for all people.[1] I am interested not so much in Ahern's argument that Karl Marx was already thinking about degrowth in the nineteenth century but in how the concept of degrowth points one way forward, toward the development of a collective consciousness that understands concentrated capital cannot continue unabated. We have seen the Titans double the value of their asset management funds in five years. Are we to allow this level of wealth concentration to continue? If we understand the problem, then we can foster a consciousness to address human inequality and wealth mismanagement.

I say wealth "mismanagement" because that is exactly what it is. The resources of the world ought to belong to humanity as a natural right of being alive. By allowing extreme inequality to exist in the world, we deny our collective humanity. We must call for the redistribution of concentrated capital to meet the minimum standard of living for all humans. This is not such a radical idea. Even the World Economic Forum is calling for a living wage as a natural right that is beneficial to businesses and workers alike.[2]

However, the difficulty is that inequality cannot be addressed by simply paying employees a better wage. We must decide to address the Titans and their forty million wealthy clients, directly asking them to reverse the continuing concentration of capital by sharing their wealth more openly. They are people with names and addresses who can be asked to make the necessary changes to end human suffering and to save what is left of the environment. We are all stakeholders in the world,

1. Andrew Ahern, "Red and Green Make . . . Degrowth: On Kohei Saito's 'Marx in the Anthropocene,'" *Los Angeles Review of Books*, July 23, 2023.
2. Reggie Ecclissato, "What's a 'Living Wage' and Why's Paying It Good for Business and Workers?," World Economic Forum, May 21, 2022.

with the right to challenge, individually and collectively, gross inequalities in the distribution of wealth. Fiduciary wealth management must include assets for human betterment, not just the maximization of return on capital. The Titans must allocate a certain percent of their wealth management capital to end hunger and extreme poverty in the world. If the Chinese can eliminate extreme poverty, then the Titans can as well. We have a moral obligation to ask them for these changes and, if they remain unresponsive, to engage in creative direct actions that get their attention in different ways.

New research shows that disruptive protests help, rather than hinder, social change, the *Guardian* reported in July 2023.[1] Guerilla protests in Britain's roads, art galleries, and public events might enrage the press, politicians, and the public, for example, but seven out of ten academics surveyed in the piece believe that strategic nonviolent protest tactics are "at least quite important" to the success of social movements.

Core social institutions within capitalist countries—including government ministries, defense forces, intelligence agencies, the judiciary, universities, and elected bodies—recognize to varying degrees that the overriding demands of Titan capital growth spill beyond the boundaries of nation-states. The resulting worldwide reach is evidence of a new form of global hegemony represented by coalitions of core capitalist nations, which engage in regime-change efforts via sanctions, covert actions, co-options, and wars that target ideologically hostile nations such as Cuba, Iran, Iraq, China, and Russia.

Global imperialism is a manifestation of concentrated wealth, managed by an elite association of several hundred

---

1. Damien Gayle, "Disruptive Protest Helps Rather than Hinders Activists' Causes, Experts Say," *The Guardian*, July 7, 2023.

people, among whom the 117 Titans examined in this book are predominant. On the opposite side stand innumerable activists who campaign for human rights, civil liberties, and democratic governance. We must stand on the Universal Declaration of Human Rights and challenge global imperialism and its fascist governments, media propaganda, and armies of empire, as fully and nonviolently as possible. Allowing the continued concentration of wealth by the Titans is a recipe for extreme poverty, environmental disaster, and global nuclear war.

Our agenda must be full resistance to the Titans of Capital. We can oppose the counter-democratic consequences of concentrated wealth by championing democratic, grassroots decision-making processes that promote human rights and protect the world's environment.

If this book helps return power to the people, then writing it will have been worth the effort.

Peter Phillips, PhD
Professor Emeritus
Political Sociology
Sonoma State University

ACKNOWLEDGMENTS

I want to first acknowledge Mary M. Lia, my wife and partner, who has unrelentingly supported me during the two-year effort to complete this book. She remains my daily adviser and loving supporter, who makes life adjustments to accommodate the many hours required for researching and writing a political sociology book. After I retired from Sonoma State University, we moved to Albuquerque, New Mexico, in 2021, where I worked on completing *Titans of Capital*.

The staff and board of Project Censored have been long-term supporters of my research on global elites. Thank you to Mickey Huff and Andy Lee Roth, who helped at every stage in the production of *Titans of Capital*; and to Shealeigh Voitl, the Project's digital and print editor, for her keen review of the book in manuscript form. Thanks also to Adam Armstrong for his continuing technological support and communication outreach. With the support of the Media Freedom Foundation, and in partnership with Seven Stories Press, Mickey and Andy established the Censored Press to publish important media-analysis books and to address how the powerful dominate and control the world. Thank you to the editorial board of the Censored Press—including Nora Barrows-Friedman,

Mischa Geracoulis, Veronica Santiago Liu, T. M. Scruggs, and Dan Simon—for its continuing support of my work.

Very special thanks to Kristen Steenbeeke, who skillfully and carefully reviewed and edited the entire manuscript, making each page not only more readable but also better all around. Thanks also to Katherine Seger for additional proofreading. And special thanks also to Tal Mancini who provided essential support and feedback during the editorial process.

Thanks to Dan Kovalik for writing the book's foreword, and to Anson Stevens-Bollen for creating its original cover art.

Great thanks to Seven Stories Press for designing *Titans of Capital* and arranging for its publication. A special acknowledgment to Dan Simon, whose belief in the importance of this work was unwavering. Thank you to Jon Gilbert, operations director; Ruth Weiner, publicity director; Stewart Cauley, art director; Claire Kelley, marketing director; Tal Mancini, managing editor; Bill Rusin, sales director; Allison Paller, web marketing manager; James Webster, web marketing assistance; Anastasia Damaskou, publicist; Silvia Stramenga, foreign rights director; Eva Sotomayor, associate publicist; Catherine Taylor, SSP UK; Oona Holahan, assistant editor; and Noa Mendoza, editorial assistant.

The Green Oaks Men's Group has been my personal weekly support network for twenty-five years and a monthly first-Friday Zoom group for the last two years. Thank you to Bill Simon, Derrick West, Peter Tracy, Noel Byrne, Dominic Favuzzi, Tom Meier, Tim Wandling, and Colin Godwin for your regular advice and suggestions regarding *Titans of Capital.*

Thank you to the Unity and Peace (UP) men's group in Albuquerque for our biweekly political discussions and sociological-analysis breakfasts. UP members include Bill Tiwald,

Charles Powell, Michael Creager, Peter Gleichman, Rick Pole, and Ric Speed.

Thank you also to the ninety friends and associates who cosigned the postscript letter from *Giants: The Global Power Elite* (2018), reprinted at the end of this book. Standing together in public and speaking truth to power, along with millions more, is vital for human survival.

Thanks to my lifelong friend Tim Ogburn, whose professional life experiences promoting economic development worldwide for the State of California have provided continuing insights as to how the global power elite control concentrated capital.

Thank you to Vietnam-era Navy Veterans For Peace activist Willard Hunter for his insight and research assistance with Chapter 6, "China: Building a Multipolar World," and his overall edit suggestions for *Titans of Capital*.

A special thanks to Justin Tiwald, professor of Chinese philosophy, University of Hong Kong, for his specific comments on Chapter 6, on China, and his overall comments on *Titans of Capital*.

I greatly appreciate the extensive research for the Titan biographies in Chapter 2, completed by Cem I. Addemir. Cem was a graduate student finishing his master's degree in communications at Illinois State University in 2023. His work was the initial layout for the biographies in *Titans of Capital*.

We must think of the future of the world in the context of our grandchildren and their grandchildren. My work is motivated by my love and concern for my own grandchildren: Katelyn Phillips, age nineteen, and Jake Phillips, age fifteen, who are entering a world where serious inequality threatens world peace and stability. I am hopeful that by identifying specifically the Titans of Capital, an awareness of inequality by both the .05 percent and the 99.95 percent will encourage positive change in the world. Global security will require an open sharing of the world's wealth, and we must expand that process by all means possible.

Thank you all,

Peter Phillips
Albuquerque, New Mexico
January 2024

2018 LETTER TO THE GLOBAL POWER ELITE

Dear Global Power Elite,

We list some 389 of you by name in this book (*Giants*, 2018). You should be honored and proud of your station in the global power structure. Being listed in this volume means you are a key part of managing, supporting, and protecting a major portion of the world's wealth. You are personally wealthy, or certainly well-off, highly educated, and have influence in multiple circles with access to vast financial resources and systems of power. Your engagement on the board of directors of one of the seventeen trillion-dollar money management firms, and/or your membership in such nongovernmental transnational policy-planning groups as the Group of Thirty, Trilateral Commission, and Atlantic Council, make you an active and influential participant in serving the interests of the wealthy 1 percent transnational capitalist class. There are many thousands of perhaps richer and even more individually powerful people in the world. We think that the 389 of you are collectively the financial and policy core of global capitalism and have the power, using your networks, to save the world from deadly inequality and pending economic or environmental chaos.

We don't have a prescription for changing the world. However, we think that addressing the world's needs in the framework of the Universal Declaration of Human Rights is a good place to start. We absolutely believe that continued capital concentration and neoliberal austerity policies only bring greater human misery to the vast majority of people on Earth. Tens of thousands of people die daily from malnutrition or easily curable diseases. Wars, covert actions, externally induced regime changes, propaganda media, and technological surveillance, all in the name of protecting the freedom to do business, is hurting humankind and will be stopped. You can easily begin that process by instituting a simple guiding principle of thinking of the future of your grandchildren and their grandchildren when making decisions on the use of world capital resources. It is no longer acceptable for you to believe that you can manage capitalism to grow its way out of the gross inequalities we all now face. The environment cannot accept more pollution and waste, and civil unrest is inevitable at some point. Humanity needs you to step up and ensure that trickle-down becomes a river of resources that reaches every child, every family, and all human beings. We urge you to use your power and make the needed changes for humanity's survival.

Sincerely,

Peter M. Phillips, Robin Anderson, Adam Armstrong, Philip Beard, Byron Belitsos, Khalil Bendib, Marty Bennett, Dennis Bernstein, Joseph Oliver Boyd-Barrett, Ben Boyington, Jacques Brodeur, Carol Brouillet, Kenn Burrows, Noel Byrne, Ernesto Carmona, Kathy Charmaz, Pao-Yu Ching, Vesta Copestakes, Michael Costello, Christopher R. Cox, Geoff Davidian,

James Dean, Michael Diamond, C. Peter Dougherty, Kristine S. Drawsky, Lotus Fong, Bruce Gagnon, Ann Garrison, Alex Glaros, Colin Godwin, Diana Grant, David Ray Griffin, Robert Hackett, Debora Hammond, David Hartsough, Janet Hess, Nolan Higdon, Kevin Howley, Mickey Huff, Dahr Jamail, Paul Kaplan, Earl Katz, Bob Klose, Valinda Kyrias, Pierre Labossiere, Susan Lamont, Elaine Leeder, Mary M. Lia, Cassandra Lista, Peter Ludes, Rick Luttmann, Wayne Madsen, Abby Martin, Concha Mateos, Miles Mendenhall, Andy Merrifield, Ralph Metzner, Mark Crispin Miller, Susan Moulton, Therese Mughannam, Mary Norman, Tim Ogburn, Jennie Orvino, Michael Parenti, Kevin Pena, Rosemary Powers, Susan Rahman, Paul Rea, Napoleon Reyes, William I. Robinson, Susan Rogers, Andy Lee Roth, David Rovics, Linda Sartor, T. M. Scruggs, Jon D. Shefner, Will Shonbrun, Laurence H. Shoup, William J. Simon, Gar Smith, Kimberly Barbosa Soeiro, Jordan Steger, Michael Sukhov, Chelsea Turner, Francisco Vázquez, Elaine Wellin, Laura Wells, Derrick West, Rob Williams, Chingling Wo, and Nicole Wolfe.

INDEX